RETHINKING POST-SECONDARY EDUCATION

Why Universities and Colleges Need to Change & What Change Could Look Like

Stephen Murgatroyd, PhD *and* **Janet Tully, MSc**
Collaborative Media Group & the Innovation Expedition Inc.
Grove Higher Education Ltd.

"The dogmas of the quiet past are inadequate to the stormy present. The occasion is piled high with difficulty, and we must rise — with the occasion".

– Abraham Lincoln, December 1, 1862

Stephen Murgatroyd, PhD FBPsS FRSA
Janet Tully, MSc

RETHINKING POST-SECONDARY EDUCATION
Why Universities and Colleges Need to Change & What Change Could Look Like

ISBN: 978-1-304-25821-2

This Book is Dedicated To

for Stephen Murgatroyd

All of those who work in universities and colleges who know that the time for change is now and who are seeking to ensure that needed change occurs…take heart – you are one of many.

for Janet Tully

All her educators, but especially Stephen who has - in the words of Albert Einstein - achieved the supreme art of teaching and has forever awakened my joy of creative expression and knowledge. There is no going back now.

Contents

Preface

There is a great deal of talk about a "transformation" taking place in post-secondary education, linked to changes in the nature of work, technology, and the challenge of financing education at a time of austerity. The New York based journalist, Thomas Friedman, for example, writing in the *New York Times*[1] in January 2013, imagined a different future for colleges and universities:

> "I can see a day soon where you'll create your own college degree by taking the best online courses from the best professors from around the world — some computing from Stanford, some entrepreneurship from Wharton, some ethics from Brandeis, some literature from Edinburgh — paying only the nominal fee for the certificates of completion."

It is through these market based mechanisms - the thinking goes - that colleges and universities will be transformed. He's still dreaming the world is flat, he can dream on.

Similar sentiments are found in a recent provocative document from Sir Michael Barber (former advisor on education to Tony Blair), Katelyn Donnely and Saad Rizvi called *An Avalanche in Coming*[2] which describes an approaching upheaval for American post-secondary education. Good luck with that.

Indeed, the combination of austerity, technology and changing demand for workers with skills is creating a context in which "revolutionary" talk and polemics is fostered and replicated without much chance for a reality check. Change is occurring, but to see these changes as harbingers of a revolution is akin to suggesting that the arrival of a new type of cheese will completely change cheese consumption in the world.

That education beyond school needs to change is beyond doubt – the issues are what changes, how, when and at what speed.

For one of us – Stephen Murgatroyd – this is not a new theme. In 1974, he (along with Stephen Thomas) published a Fabian Society pamphlet[3] in which he explored the kinds of changes needed for the emerging knowledge economy. Recently graduated from the University of Wales, both felt that, while a period of major change in the work of colleges and universities in the UK was approaching, there were little grounds for optimism. Their pamphlet ended with these words:

> *"Finally, we are not optimistic about the chances of achieving either rapid or radical reform of the kind we have advocated. It has, after all, been one of the basic themes [of the pamphlet] that the definitions of knowledge are bound up with the structural patterns of institutions. Individual academic careers, teaching roles and interests have been invested in particular and well-established methods of organization. Resistance to innovation will be considerable and understandably so."*
> *(page 16).*

For the other of us, Janet Tully has been both keen cultural observer and 'lab rat' to the changes that have been occurring in the last two decades. A Canadian born in the wilds of Canada to typical British post-war baby-boomer parents, she experienced the classic British University system at a time of significant change, when, free education was being phased out, student loans phased in, the push for all post–secondary institutions to become 'degree' granting institutions as way of bringing higher education to all and then Tony Blair's left wing government swept to power promising that "things could only get better" but ended with large scale student protests and youth disaffection. Janet offers a unique perspective on education beyond schools that crosses continents, cultures and sectors, having worked inside the post-secondary system at a Top 10 UK School and subsequently returned to Canada to change direction and sectors to advise on provincial policy towards stimulating innovation in the advanced education system.

As a Gen Xer, she has had a front row experience of change we are currently experiencing - being the generational bridge between the old guard's expectation of an education system that was free, public but also exclusive which guaranteed you a job for life; Institutions were funded by generous state taxes but also established as organizations and its ceremony, in a time well before the internet was a twinkle in Tim Berner-Lee's eye. She shares many Generation Y or 'Flux' characteristics - for whom do not see distinctions between public and private spheres, who do not understand why you cannot take a mobile device into an exam as its been part of everyday life as long as they can remember, for whom information is everywhere and not owned. The difference is she can still remember when all Apple computers were brown, not covered in aluminum (pronounced al-loo-min-nee-um).

In this short book we outline:

- Five potentially game changing developments which are having an impact on education beyond school (training, colleges, universities and life-long learning);
- Six big distractions which are getting in the way of understanding these developments and the options for change;
- Four scenarios for the future of education beyond school from the "adjustment" scenario to radical change;
- Seven key features that need to be a part of the thinking for those thinking about what needs to change; and we conclude with;
- Three major opportunities for change and thirty seven specific suggestions.

The aim is to provoke and resource a serious and mindful reflection on the possibility of change at the community, national, State or Provincial and institutional level. It is also our aim to lay out the success criteria for such change.

Our examples are predominantly Canadian – we live and work in the 'true' North (Edmonton, Alberta) – but this should be seen not as a limiting factor, but rather as a way of putting flesh on the bones of our argument. Canada in this sense is a case study.

A caution: Canada is very different in a variety of ways from the United States. For one thing, it has a much smaller population and education is entirely a Provincial (State) matter – the Federal government, with the exception of research investments, student loans and support for apprenticeship, has no role in the governance of the college or university system and does not even have a Government Ministry. For another, the Canadian college and university system has almost no significant private players – there are some, but they are small. Finally, Canada has a major demographic challenge – we will become increasingly reliant on immigration to sustain our economy (at least according to the Conference Board of Canada[4]) and this in itself will have an impact on learning after school.

Dickens wrote in *A Tale of Two Cities* that "it was the best of times, it was the worst of times" (a Canadian would have added "and it was a half hour later in Newfoundland") and this is just how many of the college and university Presidents we confer with see the present time and its challenges. This book is aimed at focusing on this being *"the start of the next of times"*.

Five Game Changing Developments for Education Beyond School

These are challenging times. Whether it is the shifting fortunes of the Eurozone, uncertainty about power and democracy and the role of community, concerns about sustainability with nine billion people expected to occupy the planet by 2050 - these appear to be difficult times. Our colleges, universities and training institutions and organizations experience these challenges directly. They impact enrollments, finances, the core knowledge they offer and teach; the support services they provide and the retention of students. They also impact their reach and sustainability.

In our view, five major developments are the most important to attend to when looking at the future of post-secondary education, lifelong learning and training: demographics, economics, technology, globalization and the changing nature of knowledge creation and dissemination.

1. Demographics

Demography is not destiny, but it is clearly shaping a great many issues in the developed world. Canada, for example, has a birth rate below replacement as do many countries in the European Union. What this means is that fewer people will be in the workforce and able to support those too young or old to work or unable to do so – less tax capacity. It also means that immigration becomes the source of new labour and the sustainability of the economy, with implications for culture, community, identity and values. As many will live longer, thanks to advances in regenerative medicine and living standards, strains will be felt in health care systems and on personal wealth. It will be the best of times for communities and the worst of times.

Growth

Since 1851, population growth in Canada has been defined by three distinct demographic periods. From 1851 to 1900, the population grew slowly by a few million. High fertility was offset by very high mortality levels. Then, in the first half of the twentieth century (1901 to 1945), despite the two world wars, the growth rate accelerated, in part due to the settlement of Western Canada. Owing to the post-war baby boom and strong immigration, the second half of the twentieth century saw the Canadian population grow at an even faster pace. During the 60 years from 1946 to 2006, Canada's population went from 12.3 million to 32.6 million, an increase of more than 20 million.

Reversal

More recently, between 2001 and 2006, Canada's population grew at an average annual rate of approximately 1.0%, mainly owing to strong immigration. This growth is expected to continue in the coming decades, and Canada could have 42.5 million inhabitants in 2056, under the most likely growth scenario using projections developed by Statistics Canada.

In 2006, international migration accounted for two-thirds of Canadian population growth. The remaining third was provided by natural increase - the growth that results from the difference between the number of births and the number of deaths. Until the early 1990s, natural increase was almost always the main engine of Canada's total population growth. However, in the mid-1990s, a reversal occurred: the migratory component became the main engine of Canadian growth, particularly because of low fertility of resident Canadians and the aging of the population. Around 2030, deaths are expected to start outnumbering births in Canada. From that point forward, *immigration will be the only growth factor for the Canadian population.*

Challenge

For colleges, universities and training organizations these demographic challenges will create a whole series of challenges:

- Demand from 18-24 year olds for *full-time* college and university places is likely to decline, as fewer young people are available to occupy such places. Also, as skill shortages in the workplace become more acute, more young people will find work more attractive than education from a purely financial point of view.
- Those who do seek training, learning and education are more likely to be part-time or full-time and working part-time and these learners will demand a great degree of flexibility.
- There will be more and more foreign trained and educated individuals seeking credential recognition (and so too will those companies looking to employ), upgrading and advanced education. In Canada, temporary foreign workers and new immigrants number in excess of 500,000 annually.
- The new learners will expect a higher degree of "systems" integration – transferability of credits, global recognition of learning, and access to support systems – than their predecessors. They are much more self and service oriented rather than institution centered.
- There will be a growing population of seniors seeking education and learning opportunities. The generation of boomers who now retiring are amongst the wealthiest retirees in the history of the planet. They will be looking for learning opportunities and new challenges – we can expect to see many new enterprises emerging from this group.
- Demand for key professions linked to an ageing population – health care, residential care, rehabilitation therapist, tourism and leisure expertise, technology support – will grow.

- There will be skills shortages – Canada is confidently predicting over one million skills related vacancies – even though unemployment may be persistently high (7-10%) for many years.

A variety of demographers have a variety of other predictions, but these are beginning to be seen as "standard" for the developed world in general (with national differences being significant – for example, Britain has a much younger population than many other EU countries). In Canada we also have the fact that the fastest growing population is our First Nations communities, both on and more likely off reserve lands (where key educational supports tied to the reserves do not follow). Historically, First Nations learners secure lower learning outcomes, lower employment and have low health status.

Institutions will need to change to respond to changing demographics. As their client base changes, so should their programming, responsiveness and flexibility.

2. Economics

Economies are changing dramatically. Growth has stalled in many parts of the world and there are various forms of economic crises, ranging from the challenge of sustaining the Eurozone, the UK's failure to tackle growth and fiscal responsibility to the slowdown in the rate of growth of both India and China. The rosy millennial forecasts now look not just like "cockeyed optimism", but wishful thinking. We are looking at a sea change in how the global economy functions.

Canada's Provinces

Canada and its Provinces are not immune to these challenges. Debt and deficit abound, with national debt at $665 billion and Provincial debt estimated at $589 billion. Together this $1.254 trillion dollar debt constitutes some 86% of GDP – close to the 90% threshold beyond which, according to some, danger lies for sustainable economic growth and development.

Provincial debt is serious for education beyond school- because unlike other nations it remains a Provincial responsibility. Compare Ontario (Canada's most populated Province) with California to get a sense of scale. Using 2010-11 figures for bonded debt, Ontario has almost $240-billion compared with $144-billion for California, even though the latter has a much larger economy and population. Once the population is factored in, California's per capita bonded debt of $3,833 is only about a fifth of Ontario's -a staggering $17,922.

Oil rich Alberta is debt free, thanks to its use of a sustainability fund (though which it has now almost completely depleted so as to balance its books). Alberta has forecast an operating deficit of between $3.5 and $4 billion in 2012-13 — at least four times what was originally predicted in the 2011-12 budget and is borrowing on the bond market to fund capital expenditures while freezing teachers' pay and cutting public expenditure. Recent natural disaster events will ensure that Alberta is unable to balance its budgets for some time.

Alberta is one of the wealthiest jurisdictions in the world as measured by GDP per capita ($52,412 per capita compared with the national average of $40,414 and a US average of $48,328). However, it appears for purely ideological reasons, the current government will not raise taxes, despite having real room to do so compared to other jurisdictions in the developed world. Instead it is cutting back on cost growth, reducing its investment in colleges and universities (a cut of 7.4% in budgets was announced in March 2013) and actively seeking roll backs in health care and K-12 salary costs.

British Columbia is also in debt – some $44.5 billion (18.6% of GDP) and is planning a balanced budget in 2013/14 by restricting growth in program spending to just 1.5%. These three Provinces – Canada's most populous robust economic engines – are symptomatic of many US States and the state of Europe. They can no longer afford the generous systems of social supports, education and health care of which they once boasted.

Government Spending

The austerity rhetoric is evident in the actions at all levels of government (Federal/National and Municipal/City & Towns). This debt load is leading to various forms of austerity measures throughout the provinces, though nothing at all like that seen in Greece, Italy, Portugal, Ireland, Spain and Cyprus. In Canada, there is a systematic and concerted effort to reduce the rise in program expenditure (actual dollars of spending, not proportional %), in general and, public salary costs, in particular (with their very rich pensions contributions).

A government generally spends its money in three key areas: the social safety net (unemployment benefits, pensions etc.); 'public goods' and services ('protection services' such as fire, police, national defense and other items like transport); and 'merit goods' and services, (education and health), these are goods that benefit the economy and society as a whole, but are hard to put a real value at point of consumption.

While the UK, for instance, will have a higher spend on the military and general government (civil service etc.), the 'merit good' spending will dominate the spend of budget. As the pie gets smaller and cuts need to be made to program spending, governments will tend to cut in those areas which are easiest to cut, i.e. those that are not enshrined in sticky legislation and red tape or a threat to the basic living standards of its population (social safety net) and less likely to cause revolt amongst the voting public (public goods). Today with aging population and the still influential baby-boomers squarely in the front and centre of political influence- healthcare spending cuts more likely to be the veritable political hot potato, this then leaves that other 'merit good' to take the cuts - education- which are seen as servicing the 'quiet' generations X and millennial.

UK Total Government Spending 2013

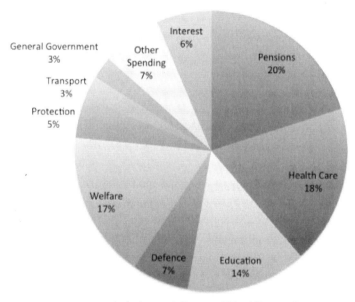

www.economicshelp.org | Source: UKpublicspending.co.uk

In contrast, the Alberta Provincial budget for 2013 had healthcare almost taking half of the actual total spend at 40%, while Advanced Education represented 6%, while K-12 Education was 15%. Even a decade ago the proportion of spending on these two merit goods were fairly evenly split.[5]

Despite this cut in real and proportional funding for colleges and universities, an economic downturn often brings benefits – people use the time of economic downturn, to upgrade skills and build their competencies so as to increase their competitive position in the workforce – but it also brings challenges. Generally, economic challenges lead governments to 'hold the budgetary line' (or even decrease) on both funding to institutions and on the fees charged to students. In some cases, cuts to funding for training, colleges and universities and other forms of student support can be expected.

However, Canadian governments have been spending more on universities and colleges than many other jurisdictions for some time. OECD data shows that, between 1995 and 2007, Canada outspent almost all nations per capita in post-secondary education except Korea and the United States. Further, Canada also devotes a higher portion of its GDP expenditure to its universities than many other countries (except Finland, Korea and the US).

At the same time, the portion of college and universities' operating costs paid for by Provincial governments has been declining over time in real terms. In part, this is because costs of running these institutions have been rising faster than inflation, and in part because of the rising costs of other government services (especially health care) have put pressure on this line of expenditure.

Even Ontario, which massively increased expenditure on post-secondary education in 2005 following a commitment to achieve a rate of 70% of its workforce holding a post-secondary qualification (deemed essential for Ontario to be able to compete in the knowledge economy), now spends less of its GDP on colleges and universities than it once did.

Challenge

Here's the challenge: between the 1970s and 2012 government funding of universities and colleges has fallen from an average of

90% of operating costs to an average of 57% - higher tuition fees have had to replace almost all of the lost funding from government.

The result – students and their families are asked to pay more. Tuition fees in Canada for 2012/13 for a Bachelor's degree cost about $6,100, with books an additional $1,300. Add in anywhere from approximately $5,200 to $7,300 for rent or residence for the eight months of college and university terms and we can see that it is a costly proposition (up to $15,000 a year plus costs of travel and food). In 2000, the core fee for the degree was $3,328 – a rise of 55% in thirteen years.

At the same time, class size has risen significantly. As colleges and universities grow in student numbers (they need to so as to fund their ballooning operating costs) then the ratio of students to full-time faculty actually worsens (from 17.5 in 1990 to 25 in 2010).

Here is a simple example of what the current economic climate means. The University of Alberta is a flagship university in Canada. It is a Top 5 University in Canada and is listed as amongst the top 100 in the world. It has 200 undergraduate programs and 175 graduate programs and is home to over 35,000 students. It has an annual budget of $1.74 billion and has an operating deficit of $15.9 million. Of its operating budget, governments (Federal and Provincial) contribute 50% - in the 1970s this figure was closer to 85%.

The University of Alberta has made cuts to its operating activities and reduced its non-core functions over the last four years since the economic downturn. It is now (March 2013) seeking a 20% cut in operations over three years and programs so as to rebalance its budget. According to its administration, it is a lean organization from an administrative and managerial point of view (though the faculty see this very differently, of course), so these "cuts" will directly affect programs, class size and ultimately the learning experience of students, who will also be expected to pay more for this "poorer" experience.

A key cost driver for universities, as for all post-secondary institutions in Canada, is salaries and the costs of energy and maintenance of physical infrastructure. The average salary of full time faculty grew at 4% annually between 2004 and 2012. In an international comparison[6], Canadian academics are the eighth highest paid at $2,526 on average (month) – behind the US ($4,638), Germany, Japan, Australia, Kuwait and the UK. Growth of the average salaried Canadian is predicted to *reach* a new normal of just 3% by 2013, though lay-offs and early retirements are now becoming a feature of the Canadian landscape. This is not necessarily a surprise when you think how Canada's institutions have to compete on a global market for talented researchers and instructors and this tends to drive up salaries, while the proximity of the US has traditionally been a lure for Canadian academic talent, tightening the market even further.

Any new investments intended to support increased access, quality and performance, generally go to increase salaries of faculty and to increase both the total number of faculty employed but also significantly add to management and administration. For instance in the US, 40 years ago there were significantly more faculty than administrators, now administration out numbers faculty by almost 2 to 1 in some places. The reasons for this are fairly straightforward: the push for universities and colleges to open their doors to the masses in the post war period and the increased 'professionalization' of delivery increased a demand for more sophisticated management tools common to most large organizations, IT specialists, accountants, alumni relations, international officers, legal departments, human resource staffers and marketing, etc. At the same time there has been an increase demand or administrative burden from delivering on external mandates from provincial governments, however in the US, the economics professor Barbara Bergmann found only a few administrators were dedicated to this function, many commentators are now pointing fingers at the administration itself as having become a function that has lost sight of what it was originally put there to do. [7],[8] At present, there is no reason to expect the same of the Canadian and the UK systems.[9]

On the basis of current trends, institutions can expect to receive a declining portion of their revenue from Governments and more from students upfront. For purely economic reasons, we can expect the next two decades to be a repeat of the last two. Funding will fall to 30% - 40% of costs from Provincial and Federal sources. Fees will rise to compensate and we can also expect to see new forms of financing involving private sector partners. The idea of a 'public education' for all who are qualified to receive it (meritocracy), is now based on the level of indebtedness an individual is willing to risk so as to secure their education, marking a shift of funding of a 'merit good' from state increasingly to the individual, who will also shift their behavior to act more like private 'consumers' rather than passive public good recipients.

On this last note, personal debt levels in Canada average 165% of income. Student loan debt in Canada is $13.5 billion, not including credit card debt and debts owed to family and friends. The debt level is rising – it has risen 33% over the last five years in the Maritimes – and will continue to rise. This leads to a significant portion of total debt (mortgage + car loans + student loans) being held by young people as they enter the work-force. It is a major challenge to the nature of learner community as well as for educational institutions-significantly affecting their choices and willingness to take risks (which is the hallmark of an innovative dynamic society).

3. Technology

 Innovations in technology have always enabled major social and economic change in, whether it is regenerative medicine which is using stem cells and related technologies to re-grow organs or restore function to failing organs or information technologies which are changing the way education is

delivered in countries that are unable to build and staff schools, technology has been transformative and disruptive. The book, music, travel, banking and communications businesses are changed forever. The ways we manufacture goods using robotics or undertake police investigations using new forensic tools are all indicators that technology is having an impact on the day to day lives of billions of people. And we haven't seen anything yet if technology futurists are right. Technology will continue to disrupt, but why should we pay attention now more than ever?

It's because of the convergence of information technology, the web and digital and social media that will have a disruptive affect on society's fabric, the way we interact and organize ourselves and our institutions. Social technologies have already enabled flash mobs to stage the overthrow of corrupt governments, the reason so many people will live in different ways and even the new way in which people meet each other for marriage, and it has the potential to be the most disruptive in education and especially advanced education whose institutions were born out of that other socially disruptive technology, the printing press; and has stubbornly remained- until recently- mostly untouched by the digital media revolution .

It would behoove us to consider the disruptive effect of print media and compare to the digital media, because the invention of the printing press did not just give us access to the cheap mass produced physical tools of books, pamphlets and cards, it allowed people to change the way they thought, organized and acted. Creating significant new ways of doing things, things that we take for granted now. Jeremy Rifkin in his book "The Biotech Century" talks about how it created the ideas of 'authorship', the idea that a single person could own an idea, it forwarded the concept of 'assembly' and standardization as printing press's letters could now be uniformly spaced and interchanged to make new ones, but it also made process thinking very linear, rigid positioning in 2D space and made the previously somewhat unreliable human oral tradition redundant. But as we move into inhabiting the digital media dominated paradigm- we're shifting to a collective authorship, flexible, customization, 3D visualization, where a 'oral tradition' is somewhat returning where people now share their thoughts and ideas orally and face-to-face but through recorded video or 'real time' social media. This is how the typical human being of the 21st century will think and behave and it will require its educational institutions to do the same.

'Adventures' in Disruptive Technology

One example of this disruption in post-secondary education is the arrival of MOOCs – Massive Open Online Courses. The term refers to a web-based class designed to support a large number of participants *who do not pay for this service*. Major universities world-wide are partnering to offer MOOCs and large numbers of students enroll in these courses – literally thousands per course (one course attracted over 150,000 learners). Typically, students enrolled in a MOOC watch video lectures – often sliced into digestible 10 or 15-minute segments – and interact with instructors and fellow participants in online forums. Some MOOCs require students to take online tests or quizzes with multiple choice answers that can be graded automatically, while others require students to complete peer-reviewed assignments; Some MOOCs use a combination of these assessments. Through challenge examinations (for which they pay a modest fee, generally less than $100), individuals who complete MOOCs may be able to obtain credit, which they can then transfer to degrees, diplomas or other credentials.

Many have seen the arrival of MOOCs as the "beginning of the end" for post-secondary education as we know it. MOOCs triggered Clayton Christensen, Thomas Friedman and others to declare transformation to be now occurring. There is, however, a substantial literature documenting the nature of "hype" with respect to technology products and services which should be attended to here. Indeed, as the following diagram illustrates, there are models built of the "hype cycle", known generally as the Gartner Hype Cycle, named after the consulting company that developed it.

Gartner Hype Cycle

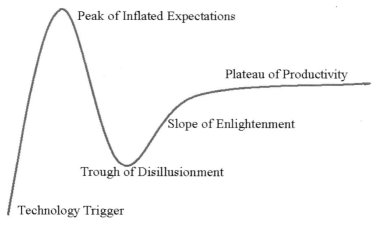

Essentially the Gartner Hype Cycle suggests that between launch and the mature use of a product (e.g. a learning management system or MOOCs) or a service (e.g. crowd sourced learning resources) a series of experiences are passed through which reduce the hype to reality. Claims made boldly at the beginning of the cycle – e.g. the paperless office, Power Point, will transform the experience of teaching in positive ways, mobile learning will change where we teach and learn – are gradually downgraded until we find a point at which the technology or service has a meaningful and productive place in our experience, usually a different and lesser place from that we originally anticipated.

A simple example of this is the power of free to use video conferencing (through Skype or ooVoo or similar services) for online learning. When Apple launched its mini Tablet in 2012 this was a major focus for the launch, together with dedicated applications for online mobile learning. While over 1 billion downloads have occurred from iTunes University since its launch in 2007, the use of interactive video on tablets or other devices for credit based learning is still nominal.

A particular distraction, at least at this time, is the positioning of learning analytics as a transformative practice for post-secondary education. Some kinds of learning analytics have been known and used since education exists, like:

- Grades and test scores.
- Student and teacher surveys of various kinds, e.g. course assessment or exit questionnaires.
- Learning e-portfolios, i.e. students assemble productions and reflect upon these (used quite a lot in professional education).
- Tracking tools in learning management systems.
- Cockpits and scaffolding used in many Computer Supported Collaborative Learning tools.
- Student modeling in artificial intelligence and education.

Modern learning analytics draws a lot of ideas from industry and its various attempts to deal with information, such as business intelligence, quality management, enterprise resource planning (ERP), balanced score cards, marketing research and web analytics. The common idea is to extract key performance indicators from both structured and unstructured data and to improve decision making. A related and important influence is a political will to articulate and measure quality standards in education leading to a culture of quantitative assessment: evidence based decision making. The new technology tools and resources are built, but their use in decision making is weak and, at the faculty member level, almost non-existent.

In part the issue is focus: faculty members, Department Heads and Deans are busy and have little time to master what are in fact overly-complex systems. But also, they see little need to change. So the second issue is the rationale for their use. The organizational leadership generally positions these tools and resources as opportunities to gain efficiencies and effective resource utilization. What the front of the organization are looking for is something different – something that will help learning to occur while making their life easier. They see the tools *as presented* as doing neither. For them, they are a distraction.

While technology always has great promise, colleges and universities have learned not to be early adopters. IT budgets are generally in the order of 4-5% of the operating budgets of institutions and they are always under great pressure. Readily embracing "the next new thing", given the Gartner Hype Cycle, is rarely a smart thing to do. And in the period since the launch of Smart Phones and Tablet devices, the hype has grown. It is a wise team that turns down the volume on the hype machine.

As we have seen in other jurisdictions – and well documented by the Commonwealth of Learning[10] - the key investment is not in technology, tablets or networks but in shifting the strategic mindsets of college and university academic leaders, building capacity of the faculty for the use of open and distance education, e-learning and open educational resources and changing the one faculty member = his or her own classes business model. Without rethinking some fundamental things, nothing much will happen.

4. Globalization

A Canadian student seeking to obtain an MBA in Vancouver is spoilt for choice. In addition to the very fine degrees they can obtain from Simon Fraser, University of British Columbia or the University Canada West in face-to-face sessions in classrooms, both full and part time, they can also study this degree online. They can do so from a variety of Canadian Universities – Athabasca for example (which is based in Alberta but offers its program nationally) – or from Herriot-Watt (Scotland), the University of Phoenix (USA) and hundreds of others from around the world[11]. The MBA is a global product offered globally to students locally – it is known as a *glocal* program.

While such programs are explicitly excluded from the North American Free Trade Agreement at this time, there is constant pressure to treat post-secondary education (non compulsory education and training of any kind) as a service sector and to see it as subject not just to educational regulation but to trade regulation.

One innovation in Australia has a number of universities who have partnered to create Open Universities Australia. This for-profit corporation offers online courses throughout Australia and Asia and does so in order to secure revenues and profit for the founding Universities.

In 2012, it is estimated that some $1 billion was invested in the private, global education business (K-PhD). In particular, MOOC providers such as Udacity and Coursera secured access to capital to enable them to "go global".

It is just a matter of time before these global aspects of the offering of training and learning has an impact on institutional strategies. But globalization has already had a significant impact in another way.

As funding from National, State and Provincial governments "shrinks" in real terms and student fees are regulated, colleges and universities see international students paying significantly higher fees, as an opportunity to make up the revenue shortfall *without* having to fundamentally change their business model. Indeed, the former Premier of Ontario encouraged such an approach when he began to reduce the rate of grant increases offered to colleges and universities in Ontario. In some departments – especially science, technology and medical research faculties – overseas students provide ongoing revenues essential to their survival – without them, there would be fewer Departments of Chemistry, Biology and Physics.

Part of the reason, then, for globalization is driven by economics – international students pay more than national students for their education. The other major driver is that the war for talent – the search for skilled and innovative employees – is global. The global war for talent is a consequence of the demographic challenges of the developed world and the fast growing, well educated population of young people from the emerging economies. It's a "marriage made in heaven", according to one University President.

With online learning being available globally and the war for talent being a global war, we can see institutions looking beyond their "catchment" for revenues, opportunities for collaboration and partnership and the more rapid movement of students around the world.

The most compelling example of these developments is occurring in the European Council – all member states are "aligning" their postsecondary education systems to permit transferability and exchange – some forty seven participating countries. It is possible for a student to start their education in one country and finish it in another without loss of credit in the process. The Bologna process, which began in 1999, is an ongoing process driven largely by a focus on competitiveness and economics. While there are many criticisms of this process, the reality is that it is blurring regional and national boundaries from a student perspective: for students in Europe, globalization is happening now.

The Europeans have been joined in this work by the Commonwealth. The thirty two Commonwealth countries which govern small states have aligned in an agreement for transnational qualifications, which in turn have been aligned with the Bologna process[12]. This means that some fifty seven countries (with others seeking to align themselves with the process) have agreed the rules for common and transferable qualifications aimed at the free movement of learners and labour mobility.

This can also be seen at a more prosaic level. Individuals seeking to qualify as Engineering Technologists or Power Engineers – a skill in high demand in a number of sectors of the economy – can use agreements made in Dublin and Sydney agreements for engineers to secure recognition of their skills and competencies in several countries[13] - trades and professional training is now a global business.

5. Knowledge Creation and Dissemination

 In 1961 Derek J. de Solla Price published the first quantitative data about the growth of science, covering the period from about 1650 to 1950. The first data used were the numbers of scientific journals. The data indicated a growth rate of about 5.6% per year and a doubling time of 13 years. The number of journals recorded for 1950 was about 60,000 and the forecast for year 2000 was about 1,000,000. His prediction underestimated the rate of growth actually experienced – we now double the rate of publication every seven years[14].

The best estimate we have is that there are around 24,000 peer reviewed journals covering all academic fields. Some 4,000 publishers produce these journals. This explosion of knowledge is accelerated by internet open source publishing and the development of a substantial, scientific non-peer reviewed literature. In addition, it is estimated that there are over 175,000 non-peer reviewed academically focused journals.

Publication in peer-reviewed journals is still increasing, although there are big differences between fields of study. There are no indications that the growth rate has decreased in the last 50 years. At the same time, publication using new channels, for example conference proceedings, open archives and online, is growing fast.

Just as in other fields, technology is changing the nature of knowledge production. For news media, more use is being made of bloggers and self-declared reporters. With technologies like Skype, video and audio recording via Smart Phones and blogging, reporting and analysis of events can now be undertaken by anybody, with or without journalism training and experience. Our knowledge of developments in the Middle East is in part informed by such sources.

In science we can also see the impact and influence of similar forces. Look at the skeptical response to the science of climatology from both some scientists with peer reviewed science who offer alternative interpretations of data than the "consensus" that man is a major contributor to global warming, but also bloggers who have relevant expertise (in statistical analysis, computer modeling for example) who are "taking on" the scientific establishment. Also look at the impact of "leaking" emails between scientists (Climategate)[15] and the role of the media in promoting a particular theory of climate change against competing theories.

More specifically, we see a blurring of a once clear boundary between science, public policy, and the political arena not just in relation to climate change, but also to other areas such as drug policy, education, health care, land management, health and safety and so on. The current role of science and the use of scientific knowledge in society are becoming a major challenge, opportunity and issue.

One feature of science which has changed remarkably is the speed at which a scientific finding can be shared with the world – and scrutinized by the world. A paper published on Monday in a peer reviewed journal published online can be "trashed" by Friday by peers, non-scientists and others and the drama of this process can be played out in blogs and on web based media. For example, the Proceedings of the US National Academy of Science (PNAS) published a paper by a group of scientists which purported to show that it was likely that the US could expect a Katrina scale event every other year[16]. Within hours, Roger Pielke Jr. (one of the leading experts in North America on extreme weather events) had offered a stinging critique, essentially destroying the argument of the paper. The original PNAS paper claimed a trend of increasing extreme hurricane events when the consensus is that there is no trend – no change in hurricane activity since 1900 (if anything, a modest decline). Within three days several other experts of hurricanes had supported Piekle's position and major newspapers ran stories about the "spat" between these climate scientists[17]. Five working days for serious science to be subject to substantial, and in this case damning peer scrutiny. Similar stories can be retold in other disciplines (especially economics[18]).

In a variety of studies of knowledge creation and development, these new networks of creation and networks of criticism have been the subject of considerable scrutiny themselves. The conclusion is that the way knowledge is produced, shared, subject to scrutiny and becomes part of the fabric of "knowing" has changed significantly since the birth of the internet and the arrival of globalized science, social science and humanities. This has a major impact on how knowledge may be taught, shared and understood – it is another factor that is challenging our conventional approaches to teaching and learning.

Looking Forward: Making Sense of the "In Between Time"

These five forces or patterns of change are the drivers of the shifts that are reshaping post-secondary education and training. They are leading to new economic realities, new power balances, new cultural realities within communities and a new focus on meaning and value and they will have a profound effect on colleges, universities and training organizations. It would be easy to be pessimistic - a common mindset for those who dislike change and would prefer to cling to the past rather than leapfrog to the future. While there are opportunities, there are also challenges.

What would help is if the future were clear - a vision and understanding of the innovation expedition it will require for us to "arrive" somewhere on the S curve of the new paradigm for education beyond school. But this vision is elusive and unclear, with many articulating a bleak view of the future. We are in between an "old" way of working and a new – the "in between time", as the following diagram shows.

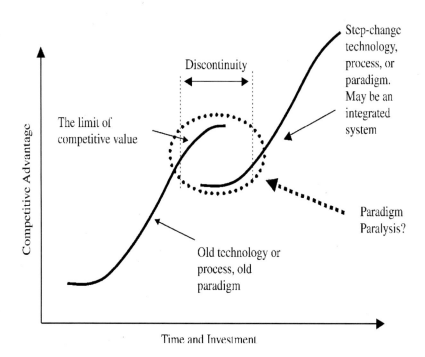

These are the elements of the kind of post-modern post-school education system we are working towards, but it will be a messy journey. We can expect conflict driven by scarcity, envy, ideology and misunderstanding. We can expect an increase in distress before we see an increase in hope. We can imagine missed steps on our journey to a different future. What we can't expect is to go back.

> **What kind of skills will tomorrow's society need?**
> Cunning thinkers required. Tomorrow's economy needs
> people that can think quickly and independently. The rapid
> pace of technology development alone has sped up the need
> *and* ability to make decisions quickly on increasingly complex
> issues. This requires an increased level of independent thought
> or never seen before in industrial workers of yesteryear- (think
> of Henry Ford's production line workers who were making
> parts for a car in any colour as long as it was black. Many of
> these jobs are now routinized by IT and robots.) In effect, it
> has had a democratizing effect on the workplace, requiring
> every individual to take a leadership role at some point in their
> workday, life and career. Therefore today's employers are
> increasingly advertising for people with creativity, initiative
> and 'good judgment'- compare this with a hundred years ago
> on the frontiers of North America, the Hudson Bay Company
> required all new hirees required to have a "good set of teeth
> and the ability to lift 150 pounds". Management guru Seth
> Godin said it succinctly in his book *Unleashing the Idea Virus
> (2000),* yesterday's economy needed people with 'hand to eye
> co-ordination', the biggest need we now have is for people
> with 'brain to mouth co-ordination'.

The future will be a contested space. There are already two "camps"
– fundamentally different ideologies – seeking to occupy this space.
One is dominant and the other finds itself on the defensive. The
dominant force is the global education reform movement (GERM)[19]
and the ideology seeking to defend itself is one driven by the notions
of equity and public good.

GERM and the Agenda for Education Beyond School

The global education reform movement is driven by a view of
education as serving the economic needs of a jurisdiction. The
language of this framework is one of competencies, skills and

knowledge needed for the workforce and to sustain and grow a vibrant and diverse economy. It is mingled with the language of business – accountability, productivity, performance and management - which is not surprising, since many of those advancing this view are corporations (CISCO, Microsoft, News Corporation, Pearson and others, who also have a stake in providing solutions to this movement). While GERM is especially strong in K-12 education, it is also now permeating training and post-secondary education world-wide.

At its heart, GERM involves these ideas:

- Learning can be broken down into competencies and competencies can be tested for using powerful and effective analytic tools.
- Learning not tied to competencies or skills needed for the economy is not worth substantial investment – creative arts, fine arts and sports are marginalized by a strong focus on science, technology, engineering and mathematics – the so called STEM subjects.
- Teachers are part of the problem not part of the solution – they need to be seen not as designers and creators of learning, but as facilitators of agreed curriculum. The idea that teachers are "professionals" gets in the way of efficiency, productivity and cost control. Teachers need to be better trained, managed and paid by the value they add to learning as measured by analytics.
- Curriculum needs to be standardized so that it is fair to all and we can test progress in standardized ways.
- Learning can and should be "personalized" – technology enables this (especially adaptive technologies), made easier when the curriculum is standardized – it makes testing and getting to scale easier.
- Teachers should make more use of technology so that they can better monitor student progress, mastery of competence

and intervene when a student is seen (from analytic data) to be struggling.

- Education should be available anytime and anywhere – technology enables this.
- Institutions should be accountable for their learning outcomes and cost management – value added auditing should be undertaken.
- All credits are equal and should be transferable.

Governments, like those in the UK, Australia and the US, are systematically pursuing GERM in their K-12 systems and this is also having an impact on training, college and university education. Underlying this is the use of business models to manage and run institutions, as if private business knew how to deliver efficient and effective public education. Institutions which adopt GERM tend to have a high manager to teacher ratio, high technology costs and at the end of the day, very little evidence of real improvements in learning outcomes.

The GERM is a paradigm which is competing for a major slice of the future of post-secondary education and the training "industry" – major venture and private investments are being made for exactly this purpose. We can thus see GERM as a vendor driven strategy which governments are finding attractive. At is at the heart of the idea of the management of education as a social enterprise rather than a public good.

Public Good, Equity and Education

An alternative framework, also competing for a major slice of the future, sees the work of training organizations, colleges and universities very differently. Rather than focusing on the "products" of post-secondary education and training in terms of the workplace and the economy, this approach sees education beyond school as an opportunity to enable and encourage the pursuit of bold, big ideas and to develop the person as a citizen, imaginer and lifelong learner.

It is also seen as a way of creating real opportunities to promote and support the public good and well-being of society and community through enhancing the ability of learners to think critically and develop a life-long passion for learning for learning's sake.

Rather than being competency driven and focused on competitive skills, this approach sees learning beyond school as a fundamental process in support of a more equitable, informed and empowered community / society in which informed and engaged citizens lead a quality of life which has meaning for them.

The key ingredients of this approach are:

- A focus on the learner as a whole person, not just as a potential employee or "contributing citizen".
- A focus on understanding, engagement, knowledge and skills – balancing these different aspects of the task of learning and understanding.
- An understanding that the key to such learning is the teacher (or team of teachers) and they must be empowered to align available resources to the needs of the learner.
- Rather than having a strong focus on accountability, this approach favours assurance and assessment focused on helping the learner improve their learning.
- The teacher and the communities of practice to which she belongs are central to this approach to learning. Rather than "follow" the script of a master course, here teachers as professionals tailor their learning designs and activities to the needs of the individuals in their class.
- In the name of equity, there is a strong focus on inclusion and accessibility – rather than continuously increasing the GPA needed to "get in" to college or university, institutions and programs look more to commitment, determination and engagement. Some institutions have abandoned selection for undergraduate level programs (e.g. The Open University UK,

Wawasan Open University Malaysia or Athabasca University Canada), preferring to focus on outcomes not inputs.

- Attention is paid to the support needs of learners – additional help is available for those struggling with concepts or skills or who needs additional help because of a learning or other disability.
- Compassion, mindfulness and empathy and support are seen to be as core to learning as outcomes.
- Technology can be used to support these overall activities, but is not "the answer".

This provides a very different philosophical base for the work of training organizations, colleges and universities – leading to very different designs for learning, assessment and curriculum.

Many attempts are being made to focus on equity not just in terms of access but also in terms of success in education – it is at the heart of the UNESCO's work on rethinking education[20], for example as well as being at the core of UNESCOs Delor's Commission four pillars of education[21]. It competes with GERM for the ideological standing as the base for strategic policy and investment decisions by Government.

Conclusion

The "in-between" time is a battleground between these two big ideas – GERM and Equity – and the battle is taking place in every jurisdiction, every Department and every funding and regulatory agency that carries a responsibility for education beyond school. Discussions are now being in the classroom, in online forums, government offices and even around the kitchen table

If we are to understand that the future is not a straight line from the past – we are in the midst of a disruption – then we need to understand the drivers for change documented here and their global and local implications.

It's these drivers and this review of the GERM versus Equity debate as a response to the emerging vacuum for the future frame the rest of this book.

The Six Big Distractions

"The future isn't what it used to be", said Yogi Berra. Our key point is that the future is uncertain and unclear – it is not a straight line from the past. We do not know what the future of education beyond school will look like, but there are clear contenders for the "prize" emerging at this time.

There are also significant distractions. In this short chapter we will look at some of these distractions – six in fact. These are: (a) the hype about technology and transformation; (b) the idea that the "rate of return" (*sic*) on the students' investment in education is in decline; (c) the "sky is falling" response to challenge, threat or change; (d) only the "big names" will survive; (e) threats to quality; and (f) students are digital natives.

The Technology Hype

We have already introduced the Gartner Hype Cycle[22] to suggest that some of the current and fanciful notions about students, technology and learning are just that – fanciful.

Whether it's the idea of mobile learning, the iTunes University (which has had a billion downloads since it began in 2007), video based learning, gamification of learning, simulation or other forms of online learning – all of which are occurring and are needed – the technology is over-hyped and over-sold.

But there are other approaches to technology which also need to be "unmasked":

1. Technology for learning and in classrooms does not automatically lower the costs of education beyond school, even if learners are asked to bring their own devices (BYOD). Technology remains a cost centre and few have found a way

of securing a high return for a college or university from the leveraging of technology.

2. Technology does not replace an instructor or teacher; rather it supplements them or provides support to the learner and instructional intentions of faculty. The key to learning for most students is the relationship the student has to knowledge, to other students and to their coach, mentor and guide (instructor).

3. Technology is ubiquitous, but students still use only a fraction of the capacity of the devices they access regularly – most students only know a small portion of the functionality of the software they use, have not been trained in effective search and analysis techniques and rarely use the reference/citation resources "built in" (or can be found as a free "app") to their devices.

4. Technology can be a distraction – how many tweets or facebook status entries occur during a single class?

5. Technology is only as effective as the person using it. For example, a 1.5 hour videoconference needs a skilled facilitator to manage the flow of the social conversation.

6. Technology stale dates quickly (every two years on average), as do the materials students can access via the technology. Who wants a version 1 iPad when version 4 or 11 is available? The minute the purchase is made, obsolescence begins. Colleges and universities used to treat the purchase of technology as a capital item and amortize that purchase over 3-5 years. Many are now writing off the purchase of some technology (lap-tops, iPads, Smart Phones etc.) in the year of purchase. They are not "assets" but liabilities.

There are positive roles for technology, as we shall see later, but seeing technology as _THE_ central part of the "solution" to the challenge of the "in between time" is a distraction.

There are two primary reasons for saying this. The first is that the adoption rate by faculty and the continued skepticism they show towards e-learning makes widespread and rapid adoption of technology based innovation unlikely. The second is that Governments, despite lauding innovation and technology in higher education, are hesitant to make the substantive, continuing and focused investments together with the regulatory and policy changes needed to enable technology innovation to drive system change. All are working in a way that ensures that e-learning and distance education remain at the margins of the "core business" of higher education.

Return on Investment for Learners

Some are suggesting that, for some learners at least, a college or university education is not worth the increasing costs that they (or their families) pay for that education. "University education no guarantee of earnings success" says a headline in Canada's Globe and Mail in September 2011[23]. Worse, we read this:

> "Maybe it's time to ask a question that seems almost sacrilegious: Is all this investment in college education really worth it? The answer, I fear, is that it's not."[24]

The argument goes like this:

- Students are paying an increasing portion of the costs of their college or university education or the costs of training –

    o   In Canada, student debt is a major feature of household debt. *Average tuition fees increased four-fold between 1990 and 2010, rising from $1,271 to $5,139. By the end of September 2010 student debt had almost exceeded $15 billion—more than the debt of some provinces. This $15 billion figure does not include approximately $5 to $8 billion in provincial student debt and personal debts such as credit cards, lines of credit, and family loans.*

- Not all students gain a life-time earnings advantage from the fact of having completed a university or college education or holding a trade's ticket/license.
- Therefore the value of the investment made in education by a student (including interest on debt) is declining when lifetime earnings are examined.

However, this argument, even though it is heard now more often than at any time in the past, is *not* very strong at all.

Data is available which looks at earnings over a life-time for those with different qualifications. Statistics Canada[25], in a 2008 study, demonstrates that a post-secondary qualification leads Canadians to:

(a) Higher incomes over time;
(b) A higher and faster ability to grow their income through promotion and mobility;
(c) Higher pension earnings; and
(d) Greater savings and assets.

It is also the case that those with a post-secondary education are less likely to find themselves unemployed.

A 2013 report from the OECD[26] also emphasizes the economic value of a higher education. In their "at a glance" report they note that, *on average* across the OECD member countries, the proportion of post-secondary degree holders who were unemployed increased by 1.5 percentage points from 2008 to 2011, to 4.8 percent, while it increased by 3.8 percentage points for individuals without a secondary degree, to 12.6 percent.

There are challenges. A 2004 report commissioned by the Ontario Coalition for Postsecondary Education[27] found that, while 25% of university grads made significantly more than their high school and college peers, another 25% of university grads actually earned *less* than the average high school graduate. A study of workers two years after graduation shows that those low-earning or underemployed university grads may have been better prepared for the workforce having taken a skills-focused college program. Much depends on what programs of study a person chooses. A degree in sociology may be more problematic than a degree in engineering from an earnings viewpoint. Given that university tuition fees in Canada currently average about $5,366 a year and average students who take a student loan to finance their education begin their working life with a debt of nearly $27,000, careful thought needs to be given to the route to the labour market.

No matter the type or cost of a degree, statistics show that post-secondary education does pay off. The premium earned for a university degree is about 40 per cent for men, and 51 per cent for women. Full-year workers in their 40s who are male, the average bachelor's degree holder earns $91,000 a year. Those with a college diploma earn $63,000, and those with just high school, $62,000. The equivalent for woman in her 40s with a bachelor's degree earns $62,000, a college diploma she will average $45,000 a year and with high school alone, $40,000. The Canadian Centre for Policy Alternatives study found because of these higher wages, post-secondary graduates pay *more* than the full cost of their education in *taxes* after graduation.

In addition to this, the *demand* for those with post-secondary education is not falling, but in fact increasing. The Canadian labour market outlook predicts that over the period to 2025, 35 per cent of all new jobs will require university education, and 42 per cent will require non-university post-secondary education. The outlook is far from being bleak for those who attain post-secondary qualifications.

"The Sky is Falling"

Faced with major change, challenge or threat how an institution or system responds is critical. In Alberta, for example, colleges and universities are facing "budget cuts" of 10 – 20% over the next three years. For some, usually those whose program is about to be cut or the faculty or management team about to be laid-off, this is "the end" – "the sky is falling" – and, to some extent it is.

But the concern to preserve the current situation, the *status quo pro ante* inevitably starts a debate and creates a lot of noise, but which in turn *not* to good outcomes, but generally leads to compromise, half-hearted change implementation and poor decision making. The "sky is falling" rhetoric is a distraction.

The underlying voices of this distraction are these:

- *"If we do what we always do we can surely secure different results – results which will surely be game changing".*
- *"If only everyone else would change their mind (about cuts, about strategy, about the nature of learning beyond school), then we could become the program and faculty we have always wanted to be".*
- *"I understand that the economic situation demands cuts, but can't we make them somewhere else"?*
- *"The change is too deep (the cut too big, etc.) can't we make many more minor cuts over a longer period of time"?*
- *"We have tried all of these "innovations" before – they will not work".*
- *"Students really want what we have always done".*
- *"We should try weather this out – I am sure a new Government (Minister, economic reality) is just around the corner".*

However, the usual voices supporting these kinds of statements about change are those with most to lose and those with a vested interest in the status quo. Many are indifferent unless it directly and with some immediacy hits them.

In the face of a major challenge, threat or change, one of the keys to success is visionary leadership - which takes decisive and quick action and uses the challenge to make changes which, in their estimation, will lead to long-term gains. In this situation seeking to accommodate the "sky is falling" voices will delay positive action and water down the response until it becomes ineffectual or even damaging.

These voices are the *contrapreneurs* - they are very enterprising at inhibiting, stalling or preventing change. They will use a range of devices to sustain the "sky is falling" position, such as chairing key task forces, offering to analyze data, agreeing to make change happen and then delaying doing so. It is unfortunately a characteristic of some of our institutions of learning have taken contrapreneurship to both a science and an art.

Transformation – Only the Big Names Will Survive

Nathan Harden has suggested that MOOCs and the arrival of related educational services (especially learning analytics) mean the end to an array of small "no name" institutions – training centres, colleges and universities which are known locally and to their students, but which have no major regional, national or international "brand presence". Writing in *The American Interest* in January 2013, Harden said[28]:

> "The live lecture will be replaced by streaming video. The administration of exams and exchange of coursework over the internet will become the norm. The push and pull of academic exchange will take place mainly in interactive online spaces, occupied by a new generation of tablet-toting, hyper-connected youth who already spend much of their lives online. Universities will extend their reach to students around the world, unbounded by geography or even by time zones. All of this will be on offer, too, at a fraction of the cost of a traditional college education… "and also

> "…Prestigious private institutions and flagship public universities will thrive in the open-source market, where students will be drawn to the schools with bigger names. This means, paradoxically, that prestigious universities, which will have the easiest time holding on to the old residential model, also have the most to gain under the new model. Elite universities that are among the first to offer robust academic

programs online, with real credentials behind them, will be the winners in the coming higher-ed revolution."

A similar position was taken by Clayton Christensen, one of the leading thinkers about disruptive innovation in education, who has written:

> "Price-sensitive students and fiscally beleaguered legislatures have begun to resist costs that consistently rise faster than those of other goods and services. With the advent of high-quality online learning, there are new, less expensive institutional alternatives to traditional universities, their standing enhanced by changes in accreditation standards that play to their strengths in demonstrating student learning outcomes. These institutions are poised to respond cost-effectively to the national need for increased college participation and completion."[29]

Because of their brand and ability to attract the best teachers and researchers, the best instructors, the most students and the most revenue (grants, donations, etc.) will go to the known names who will soon "outpace" the no-names in their ability to leverage GERM (with a little bit of equity thrown in) to dominate the market. Doing so will squeeze out the smaller, inefficient and less recognized institutions. Small, local institutions will be a thing of the past. Students will naturally move to the best, affordable online option.

However, Harden and others are assuming that the market for learning is a perfectly competitive market and that other factors do not have an impact on the choices individuals make. Cost, proximity to family, sports related factors, peer networks and many other factors impact choice as does the level of available support. The quality of instruction is one variable among many that lead students to chose small, local "no-name" brands. Critical amongst these variables are peer networks. Many go to college or university to sustain their peer networks – learning is way of doing so.

While brand is important, especially for those seeking a career in research and academia, the majority of students are seeking knowledge, experiences, skills and competencies that matter to them and they don't necessarily have the same care for 'brand recognition', they wish to learn and to do so amongst their peers and their social networks.

Also seeking to build brand and to "out-compete" other institutions is a traditional neo-classical economics view of how a post-secondary system might work. Promoting access, opportunity and affordability speaks to a more sustainable and equitable focus for the system. Students make choices for a variety of reasons and many chose to stay at home and study rather than "leave"; they also chose to study by a combination of methods – in class, online, long form and short form courses – so as to provide flexibility and the opportunity to work whilst learning. While institutions will look for efficiency, they need not fear their pending demise from the development of online learning on their 'brand'.

Quality

Faculty members and academic leaders are fond of citing quality as a key concern, when change is proposed. It is valid preoccupation when trying to ensure the delivery of a product as so intangible and difficult to compare as a person's learning, yet has such an impact on an individuals and society's well-being. Many mechanisms have been created for quality oversight and review – quality assurance models exist and are enforced, though they do vary between jurisdictions.

But what is quality in post-secondary education? Quality is generally defined in this sector in terms of standards and requirements. This "standards" based quality approach permits some jurisdictions to "badge" programs and institutions as quality assured - the veritable 'rubber stamp'. In the US, accreditation processes developed by regional accrediting bodies or by bodies dedicated to particular disciplines, such as business school programs, have published procedural standards and process standards that "assure" us that "quality processes are practiced" here.

The core of this approach is to require the following features within a college or university, both at the level of the institution, the level of a faculty or department and at the level of a program.

Features required for quality 'rubber stamp':

- Thorough process specification, including the publication of standards and expectations, both at the level of programs and at the level of the institution;
- Audit and review of whether or not the standards and processes are being followed;
- Systematic measurement of outcomes and student satisfaction and formal processes for appeal;
- Exceptions management – what happens when problems arise?;
- Periodic independent review by peers of both student services and programs.

If you consider this for a moment, this is a very administrative, procedural, input based conception of quality, borrowed from the specific industrial model (ISO 9000). It does not reflect what the learner as customer (and funder) is actually thinking of when they talk about quality of their experience of learning. Learners are concerned with *their experience of learning*, the quality of the instruction they receive, their engagement with peers and their instructors, the volume and pertinence of the work, turnaround time for feedback on assignments, the quality of feedback, value for money, flexibility of the institution, transfer credit arrangements, acceptance of prior learning and, to some extent, the social networks they create. The institutional view of quality is increasingly misaligned with the learner *"as customer"* view of quality. As students are asked to pay increasing sums and upfront for their education, their conception of quality now rest more with a retail or 'consumer' view: *"is the item I've paid for "fit for my purposes" and how responsive is the institution when I indicate my concerns?"*

This alternative conception of quality is one that gives emphasis to:

- Student engagement and the extent and value of their interaction with faculty and peers
- Faculty satisfaction with their conditions of practice and their ability to convey the "power and beauty" of learning and understanding
- The impact of a learning experience on the student and their understanding and competence – sometimes known as the "value added" from a learning experience
- The outcomes of learning in terms of competencies and skills, knowledge and understanding

While those promoting the "standards" view of quality will suggest that these are implicit in their approach, this *is* exactly the problem. They *are* implicit not explicit. These four features should be the key *focus* for quality, not following procedures: the procedures are a means to the ends not the ends themselves.

Quality is included here as a distraction for two reasons. First, it is often cited as a reason why innovation cannot occur – "quality would be in question". Second, *quality as currently practiced* distracts administrators and faculty members because our current approach to quality is bureaucratic, time-consuming and is experienced as a distraction by many of those who are engaged in the compliance work quality requires.

For example, when did we last review in a meaningful and focused way our assessment practices or our use of projects as a basis for learning? When did we last see the low completion rates for PhDs as a quality issue rather than "students were just not up to it" issue?

When did we last look systematically at student based indicators of quality – how they judge their experience – as the critical drivers for a quality assessment?

If a large number of students fail a course, like statistics, it will often be said that the course is a high quality course, but the students are not. But a course with a high failure rate is, by definition not 'fit for purpose', a low quality course. If the intention of the course is to enable all who take it to understand and use statistics and most who register in the course fail to be able to understand and use statistics, the course is failing to deliver to the very people who have paid for it. Yet most of the approaches we take to standards based quality would say that the course has been through the quality assurance process. This is why quality is a major distraction and block to actual quality improvement. Failure rates rarely lead to a complete rethink of processes or instructional design.

We are not alone in making these observations. Despite so many fat years, universities and colleges have done little until recently to improve the courses they offer. Spending is driven by the need to compete in league tables that tend to rank almost everything about a college or university except the (hard-to-measure) quality of the graduates it produces. Roger Geiger of Pennsylvania State University and Donald Heller of Michigan State University show that since 1990-2010, in both public and private colleges in the US (it is no different in Canada), expenditures on instruction have risen more slowly than in any other category of spending, even as student numbers have risen[30]. Yet the period 1990-2010 saw the strongest focus on quality assurance as at any time in the history of these institutions. Quality assurance as now practiced is essentially driven by the need to confirm and adjust the status quo *post ante*.

Students are Digital Natives

The term "digital natives" and "digital tourists" were two terms popularized by Marc Pensky in the early 2000s[31]. Digital natives are those who are so familiar with digital technologies that they can use them with fluency, facility and creativity that others can't – the technology is a utility to them. Digital tourists have limited facility because they occasionally use technology – like Microsoft Office products or video streaming and editing products – and have some, albeit limited functional knowledge.

There is a suggestion floating amongst those who seek to influence public policy that the coming generation of students are *all* digital natives and that they will, because of their fluency, demand more and more technology for their learning and that "we had better catch-up" or be out of business.

There are several issues emerging here with this view. Here are three:

- These categories are not fixed in generational terms: as is widely attested, there are plenty of retired-age people who have great facility with digital technologies, and spent large amounts of time online, and plenty of teenagers who struggle with them and find them overwhelming and alienating- and the particular application to students starting at university or college is particularly problematic: the proportion of mature students is not negligible and is rising.
- This kind of simplistic language attributes "unchangability" to one's approach and use of technology. One cannot aspire or attempt to become a digital native: one either is or one isn't. There are plenty of people who come to digital fluency at a later stage in life than infancy. Also, some are fluent in one aspect of technology use (writing) but not with others (drawing, animation, using technology to create music).
- This language unhelpfully sets up an insurmountable barrier of incomprehension between teachers (by definition digital

tourists or new immigrants) and learners (by definition digital natives).

In colleges and universities around the world, help-desks exist to support learners and instructors who find the technology beyond them. A recent short article in MacLean's magazine[32] tells stories of what this work is like, including the story of the student who did not know how to transfer files, so they printed their essay off on the desk top printer at home and came to the college and retyped it on a computer there. An hour talking with a help desk team at any institution will tell you that the idea that *all* students generally are highly skilled in their use of technology is "nonsense" (or words to that effect).

Conclusion

Harden writes[33]:

> "Big changes are coming, and old attitudes and business models are set to collapse as new ones rise. Few who will be affected by the changes ahead are aware of what's coming. Severe financial contraction in the higher-ed industry is on the way, and for many this will spell hard times both financially and personally. But if our goal is educating as many students as possible, as well as possible, as affordably as possible, then the end of the university as we know it is nothing to fear. Indeed, it's something to celebrate".

He may be more right than wrong, but the idea that this will happen quickly and dramatically, which the rest of his writing implies, is somewhat fanciful and maybe exaggerated for the sound byte. There are many distractions and challenges and many vested interests still at play, one being an institution's 'genetic inheritance'.

The DNA of a college or university is not only similar across institutions; it is also highly stable, having continuously evolved over hundreds of years. Replication of this "academic" or "polytechnic" DNA occurs incessantly, as each retiring employee or graduating student is replaced by someone screened and judged against the same criteria applied to his or her predecessor. The way things are done is determined not by individual preference but by institutional procedure written into the genetic code and reinforced by a "standards" approach to quality and accountability.

There is evolution in the post-secondary institution, though its mechanism typically is not natural selection of random mutations. As a general rule, the institution alters itself only in thoughtful response to significant operational needs and financial or brand based opportunities. Entrepreneurism occurs within fixed bounds; there is rarely revolution of the type so often heralded in business or politics. Colleges and universities are exceptionally good at distracting agents of change and in this sense are resilient to social, cultural and political change. This is why they remain "Institutions" in words and operations.

However, the distractions described here have secured a delay in change for some time, in a time of even more rapid change. In particular, the quality distraction and the "sky is falling" are often strong fear based ways of stopping innovation and change in its tracks. The question now will be whether or not the five forces of change we examined earlier will be sufficient to overcome the inbuilt resilience of the institutions.

The good news is that student choices will change some aspects of these institutions. Demand for conventional classroom based learning in North America is growing, on average, at 1.5-2% while demand for online learning is growing between 12 and 15%. The number of part-time learners is growing as are the number seeking transfer credit and recognition for work-based learning and their own competencies. The fiscal context has changed significantly since 2007 and the "big reset" recession. The conditions may now be right to foster innovation.

Four Scenarios for Change

Scenario planning is a systematic approach to understanding options for the future. Some use this approach for "small" projects, such as the future of a specific enterprise or organization, while others use it to examine the long view of a particular aspect of society – energy, health care or education. We are using it here to look at the future of learning, training, colleges and universities in the developed world[34]. At the heart of our analysis are two key dimensions: (a) the nature of access to the learning process (where learners learn and how they secure recognition for that learning); and (b) the nature of the learning process itself (what and how learners learn) through instruction and assessment.

Dimension 1: Accessibility

All engaged in education beyond school, whether the focus is on training or advanced research skills have a concern with access to learning opportunities. There are several dimensions of this concern:

- **Who has access** – is access restricted in some way by financial concerns, class or patronage? Britain, for example, engaged in a serious government campaign aimed at ensuring that those from poorer backgrounds secured access to Oxford and Cambridge in sufficient numbers to demonstrate that these institutions were not positively discriminating against the working class. This wasn't an issue in the 1920s, but is a current policy concern[35].
- **Who has access to what** – it is not just that a person is able to secure a training place or a place in college or university, it is what kind of place and under what conditions this opportunity is "given". For example, access to elite universities has been, for many at least, a matter of securing a sufficient grade in various admissions tests (High School Diplomas, GED's, GMAT and so on). In western culture, institutions are deemed successful when they turn away more

students than are accepted. The challenge, from a policy perspective, then becomes one of "layers of provision" – different grades of institutions or programs based on input measures.

- **The cost of access** – what is the price of training, apprenticeship, certificate, diploma or a degree? The question of affordability and debt has already been raised (see pages 36-37 above) and is linked to an understanding of net present value of the learning – if I spend $27,000 now, will it produce a return on capital? Governments and institutions seek to provide some support for the most able who appear to have access to the least funds, but scholarships, bursaries and awards do not remove the challenge of cost for anything like the majority of learners.

- **Access and quality** – there is a widely understood view that the more difficult an institution is to get into then the better the quality of the education will be. This makes the assumption that inputs drive quality. They are one factor. More important, as we indicated above, are student engagement, faculty commitment, the nature of pedagogy and the currency of the knowledge in use (i.e. the link between research and teaching)? Institutions which have no restrictions on admission (i.e. open universities, such as The UK's Open University or Canada's Athabasca University) can also have high quality teaching and learning. There is no *necessary* connection between admission policies and quality *at the level of the students' experience* – this is more about brand.

We envision a dimension of change that looks at open access (no admission requirements other than payment of some kind of fee) at one end of the dimension to highly selective at the other. The reason we suggest this as a key dimension is that there are a number of developments taking place which suggest this as a critical factor for the future. These include, but are not limited to:

- **Massive Open Online Courses (MOOCs)** are open admission. Anyone can take the course (there is no admission process) and courses are free, with a modest cost for those seeking to subsequently obtain credit through some kind of proctored assessment.
- **Globalization** – it is possible to live in a remote community, such as regions of the Arctic, and study programs from a range of universities around the world with varying levels of entry requirements. The Bologna process in Europe, for example, enables this within the EU and the University of the Arctic or Open Universities Australia are examples of a collaborative institution with courses and programs from a range of providers.
- **Transferability** – students can take courses from one institution (e.g. with open admission, such as Athabasca University in Canada) and transfer them to many other places. Up to 50% a degree program can be secured this way and there are considerable pressures to permit much more transferability.
- **Equity** – jurisdictions that commit to equity as a driving principle seek to make access as open as possible.

Politically, and from the learners' point of view, access and affordability are key issues. With a global war for talent and changing demographics, the pressure to look at this dimension will be intense.

Dimension 2: The Nature of Instruction and Assessment

Historically, colleges and universities have offered programs of study defined locally by faculty, sometimes with reference to the requirements for accreditation from professional bodies (e.g. medicine, nursing, business and accounting). Faculty determines *what* and *how* a program of study will be taught and the faculty determines how the learning associated with a course within that program will be assessed. Faculty also determines *when* courses in the program will be offered and the faculty determines who amongst them will teach what when. Learners are expected to be compliant.

This model is being challenged by a variety of developments:

- **A Shift to Competency** – many institutions are now looking at breaking the learning required to obtain a credential of any kind into required competencies. Rather than focusing on instruction, the challenge the learner faces is to demonstrate that they have the competency required. This is leading to an increased use of PLAR, competency based assessment in colleges and universities and work-based learning accreditation. The Kentucky college system, for example, is breaking down all of its courses into competency units and offering some instruction for each competency unit (2-3 weeks of learning) as preparation for a pre and post-test of competency. A learner, who passes the post-test, *whether or not they have undertaken any instruction*, is given credit recognition for the competency. Similar developments are occurring at Western Governors University.

- **A Shift Away from Time Based Programming** – a variety of institutions permit learners to take courses "on demand" (Kentucky) or at more frequent intervals than a semester based system (e.g. Athabasca University's undergraduate courses start at the beginning of any month). Not only can learners start when they want to, they can call for assessments and examinations when they are ready. This changes the "time served" basis for many models of learning and instruction. This shift is greatly aided by the growing number of asynchronous courses available online.

- **Significant Growth of Online Learning** – over 6.7 million US students were taking at least one online course during the fall 2011 term, an increase of 570,000 students over the previous year[36]. In Ontario – Canada's largest Province, some 500,000 registrations occur each year in the 18,000 online courses available in that province from its own institutions.

Demand for online learning is growing at between 10-12% per annum in the developed economies of the world, while demand for traditional face-to-face instruction is growing at between 1.5 – 2%. These data do not include the massive growth in registrations in MOOCs.

- **The Growth of Blended Learning and the "Flipped Classroom"** – a sign that pedagogy in training and post-secondary education is changing is the emergence of new models of instruction on campus which fully integrate offsite (online and project based work) and in-class activities. Known as "blended" learning or "the flipped classroom", these approaches shift the learning of content to outside the classroom and the use of content (demonstrations, projects, presentations, etc.) to class time. The idea is to make the most use of faculty as coaches, mentors and guides rather than "instructors".

- **Growth of Work Based Learning (WBL) and Prior Learning Assessment and Recognition (PLAR)** – PLAR and WBL means that learners are recognized as having mastered a body of knowledge or a range of skills through their ability to demonstrate this mastery. This may have involved them taking a course of study or an agreed program of work, but may not. Several colleges, universities and training programs are now increasing the range and type of WBL accredited programs (for example, Middlesex University) and PLAR. Faster processing of international student's claims to credit is also aiding this development.

- **Personalization of Learning** – Adaptive learning technologies are enabling learners on individual courses to shape the way they receive learning materials so that they better match their learning style. With the ability to chose when they learn, how they learn and the ability to transfer their learning, learners are able to personalize their learning pathways to suit their circumstances. Increasingly, the combination of technology and human resources are leading to a more personalized learning journey for learners.

- **e-Portfolios** – an emerging practice in many institutions involves the use of learning pathways (routes to completion of a program chosen by the learner) with records of progress and samples of work being recorded in a learners own e-portfolio. Such records include transcripts of grades and course completions as well as samples of work, especially projects and presentations in which the learner was involved.

- **Automation of Assessment** – EdX, the non-profit company offering MOOCs from Harvard and MIT, has made available[37] an artificial intelligence engine that can mark assessments, both multiple choice and short essay text assessments and do so instantly. This could reduce the burden of assignment grading for Faculty while permitting students to receive instant feedback, enabling them to "redo" their assignments quickly so as to improve their performance. There is a growing discipline of adaptive educational assessment which leverages technology, machine intelligence and a range of adaptive technologies to design powerful and meaningful assessments which will transform how students are assessed, how frequently this occurs and how feedback is provided so that assessment *for* learning rather than *of* learning becomes the norm.

For many, the shift in the nature of courses, pedagogy and assessment is coming slowly. For others, it is far too fast. Faculty remain skeptical about many of these developments, with less than 30% seeing online learning as equivalent to in-classroom based learning (yet, in the Sloan Consortium study, seventy-seven percent of academic leaders rate the learning outcomes in online education as the same *or superior* to those in face-to-face[38]).

Scenarios for the Future

These two dimensions (access and instruction/assessment) appear to be shaping the debate about the future of training, college and university education. When placed together, as we have done in the figure below, we see four possible scenarios for the future. We will introduce each of the four scenarios and then discuss the challenge of strategic decision making for the sector. The four scenarios are:

1. Credit Focused Institutions
2. Program Focused Institutions
3. Merit Based Institutions
4. Elite Institutions

To some extent, these are abstract models derived from our scenario planning, but for each we can see existing organizations and players making significant strategic moves. Institutions in the "real world" are combinations of these four frames. In "translating" what follows to specific institutions ask "which of the four frames is the dominant strategic mode driving the investments and work of the organization?"

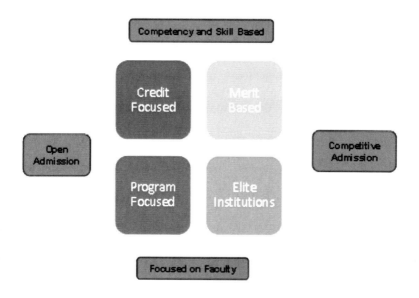

Scenario 1: Credit Focused: Awarding Credit as the Basis for a System

A key opportunity exists for an institution to be created that does little more than assess learning in terms of competency, knowledge, understanding and skill. That is, rather than teach programs and courses, this institution recognizes that the primary strategic advantage it possesses is the right to award credit. This can be for any level of learning – apprenticeship, training, college Diploma or university degree.

Such an institution would be neutral to the question of where the learner developed their mastery of knowledge, skill or understanding. Whether this occurred through "paid for" learning at a college; through their study at a training organization; through work or through self-study; the question being asked is simple: Can the learner demonstrate that they have the knowledge, skills and understanding required to be granted the credit they are seeking?

At the present time, largely for financial reasons, credit awarding is tied to established institutions, who in turn have largely tied the award of credit to the completion of *their* courses. Reluctantly, at least in most systems, they have accepted a restricted number of credits from third parties (prior learning assessment, work-based learning for credit, transfer, challenge exams) and have controlled "brand" quality through residency requirements – a requirement that students take courses at their own institution, normally 50% of a program or higher[39]. But this could change.

In the US, the American Council on Education (ACE) has credit granting rights independently of any institution or program. Credits awarded by ACE are transferable to any post-secondary institution. ACE is currently offering credit for MOOC completers who sit a proctored challenge examination which they oversee. They also undertake PLAR and WBL assessments. This kind of organization represents part of the future we imagine in this scenario.

Here is what this scenario could look like:

- Learners file a learning plan with a credit granting agency. Such plans follow consultation with plan advisors and careers specialists who help identify appropriate routes to learning, following a skills assessment, for their chosen interest.
- Learners use an online tool which helps them identify how they could meet the requirements of their learning plan – in class, online, blended learning, MOOCs with assessment, self study, mentoring and coaching – whatever is appropriate for that person.
- As learners come to believe they have mastery over a body of knowledge, a skill or have an understanding of key ideas, they call for a credit assessment.
- Their credit granting agency arranges for a credit assessment (exam, challenge activity, proctored process or whatever is deemed appropriate for that competency) and, if they are successful, enters that information in their e-portfolio. If they have completed a course which had credit assigned to it from an institution accredited by the credit granting agency, that credit is entered into their e-portfolio.
- Once they have completed their learning pathway journey, they are eligible for an appropriate diploma, degree or certification from an institution which is participating in this process.

Some things are clear about this model:

1. It is driven by learners *not* by institutions.

2. It is focused on outcomes, not time on task or courses or programs. The award of credit and certification is based on demonstrated knowledge and skill, not time served. While courses are one way in which credit can be acquired, the

credit agency has no significant interest in how the learner secured their knowledge, understanding or skill.

3. It permits total flexibility for the learner. If the learner seeks to complete their program using self-study, MOOCs and a coach then they are treated no differently at the time of assessment from those who completed their studies entirely at an institution. Given that there is no "residency", this freedom will be considerable.

4. It is market-driven. Learners determine by their choice of pathway and methods of preferred instruction how they will use all of the available services world-wide.

5. For this to work, any costs which the student incurred would be met by the learner and any institutional revenues would accrue from a combination of credit awarding, courses and programs and revenues from sponsorship. The current funding model – based on the Carnegie unit (an 'hours of study'-based unit developed in 1906) – would not be fit for purpose.

There are downsides to this model. These immediately come to mind (though there are others):

1. Institutional resistance in the name of "quality" – "We have raised quality as one of the big distractions in the debate (see pages 42-45 above). Institutions use quality as a "weapon". In most uses of the term, quality refers to fitness for use – not some abstract notion of quality of "one who dwells in the groves of academe". What institutions are actually referring to is *integrity* of the qualification *as judged by them*. Quality processes in institutions – and we have reviewed many of them for quality assurance organizations – are generally **not** focused on the experience of the learner, but on following procedures and undertaking infrequent peer review of intentions. Rarely does the teaching of a particular instructor

or Professor be reviewed, rarely does the experience of the learner matter – what matters is that procedures have been followed for the inputs into a course or program and that there are adequate procedures for assessment. Quality in this narrow sense will be used to argue that a "rag bag" of courses taken from a variety of institutions hardly makes for a quality learning experience – they will miss the "other" aspects of education, i.e. the 'experience' which are found on campus and online when the courses are all taken at *their* institution.

2. The emergence of "rogue" providers. Degree and diploma "mills" are a problem. They already exist and can be difficult to quickly locate and close. This is why a key role for a credit awarding body is to determine the conditions under which credit can be awarded. By focusing not just on transfer, but on outcomes "rogue" players will soon be found. All the credit awarding organization has to do is establish proctored challenge examinations and assessments when there is doubt.

3. Poor pathway planning and learner supports. A more serious concern is that the model relies heavily on high quality planning at the front end of the process by the learner. That is, they need to define intentions and pathways for achieving these intentions need to be established. When learners change their mind – as they do – new pathways need to be identified and mapped against the "last pathway" the learner was pursuing to maximize credit opportunities. Learning pathways need to reflect both what is available (locally, regionally, nationally and globally) and what will be acceptable to professional bodies, regulatory authorities and others. Poor planning and poor supports for planning would make this model weak for many learners.

4. Access to student funding would be problematic. Most funds for learners – both those paid direct to them as loans, grants and scholarships and those paid to institutions to support

them – are based on time not outcomes. The system is built around "the Carnegie unit".

> **What is The Carnegie Unit?**
> Colleges and Universities receive payments in many jurisdictions on a calculation of credit hours per registered student ('per –head'). A unit of credit equates to three hours of student work per week (1 hour lecture plus 2 hours of homework OR 3 hours of lab) for 16 weeks. Most courses at universities are 3 credit courses (3 hours of lecture and 3 hours of study). Students who are registered on a particular date (often part way through a semester – e.g. October 20th or February 5th) "count" for financial reasons so as to take into account drop-out. Originally developed over 100 years ago, in the early 20th Century by the then new Carnegie Foundation and at the time the first mass-produced cars rolled off Ford's production lines. The Carnegie unit is about time served ('bums warming seats'), not competency or completion.

Scenario 2: Program Focused, 'Open Admission' Institutions or Networks

In this scenario, there are no admission constraints – any student committed to learn may do so. They do so at a "host" institution from which they will graduate or complete but do so by pursuing agreed programs of study. This is currently practiced by Athabasca University (Canada) and The Open University (UK) and several other "open" universities and colleges around the world.

> **What Makes an Open University open?**
> An open college or university is an institution that has no requirement of prior 'formal' or traditional qualifications for admission to a program. Athabasca University, for example, does not require a High School Diploma or any other academic entrance qualification to be admitted to an undergraduate degree. Customized support is also given to learners who need additional time to complete or require additional tuition or remedial assistance. Open universities make it easy to enter but completion of courses and programs still require a demonstration of clear achievement of competence.

Further, to be truly open there are no residency requirements – the requirement that a certain number of courses must be taken at the "host" institution (usually 50%) – and a strong encouragement to transfer credits, review prior learning and accreditation (PLAR) and support work-based learning (WBL) initiatives. It is very similar to the previous scenario, but the key difference is that the learner is committed to working with a particular host institution and within the boundaries of their specific program offering.

This has the advantage of:

1. Leveraging existing infrastructure, though it changes the functionality of the institution which is more of a program provider and broker than hitherto (the end of residency ensures this).
2. Provides a clear route for funding the learner and the provision of program based learning. A combination of public, private and student based funding could be used to support programs in demand. Other programs in low demand would need to be supported by revenues earned by the institution or through sponsorship as is currently the case.
3. Programs would need to be more responsive to demand and would therefore be strongly tied to local and regional economic and social needs.
4. Systematic approaches to prior learning assessment and recognition and work-based learning accreditation would need to be developed across institutions.
5. Program integrity is assured because the institution determines the "rules" and "pathways" of their own programs.
6. Institutions would need to become increasingly expert at flexible provision to attract learners and sustain programs.

The downside of this scenario is that it creates significant uncertainty for an institution and inhibits innovation, as we will see in the comments below.

Here are some of the limitations:

1. The end of residency will trigger issues of "quality" from institutions – "how can a program which is a collection of credits from a variety of institutions carry our imprimatur when we have not quality controlled at least half of the credential?" will be the cry, despite the fact that the PLAR and WBL credits granted come from that institution.
2. Institutions would be even more risk adverse has very little 'risk capital' with which to launch and develop new programs, even though they may be in demand.
3. Seasonal variation in demand for programs may make it difficult to retain quality faculty – tenure and academic freedom (relevant to universities) may be comprised by the focus on demand-driven program offerings.
4. Driving a significant portion of college and university funding by outcomes will make balancing research and teaching (a key aspect of universities) difficult. Research activities would need to be funded in a separate and distinct "envelope" from teaching.
5. The varied level of learners entering the system would create issues about the level of support learners need to be successful. A learner entering a program with a low level of knowledge will need different levels of support from a learner who is already proficient in a great many of the key constructs and skills needed for success in that program – open admission has student support consequences.

Nonetheless, this scenario is becoming a key scenario for governments around the world. One could look at the general direction the EU is taking as reflecting a growing commitment to this scenario. For example, ET 2020 – the European Union's strategy for life-long learning[40] – commits to learner mobility within and between EU nations, transparency and outcomes based learning and a strong commitment to transferability of credit. While it is not explicit about open admission (it commits to working on "quality" not openness), it implies a growing commitment to open boundaries, learner mobility and more flexible learning pathways.

The Indira Gandhi National Open University has over 1.4 million students. India also has thirteen state open universities. Malaysia, Nigeria, Hong Kong, China and many other countries have developed successful open universities and colleges. Open education is thriving.

Both of these first two scenarios put the learner in the driver's seat not the institutions, though this second scenario gives institutions more of a presence in the choices learners make. While the first scenario creates a complex market with a credit granting agency acting as a kind of "stock exchange", this second scenario gives credentialing power to institutions. In particular, it gives power and authority to the faculty peer review process to determine what counts for credit. That is, faculty in this scenario retain some significant decision authority, but much less (because of the ending of residency and the requirement for open admission and transferability of credit) than is the case either at this time or in scenario four, to be described shortly.

Scenario 3: Merit Based Admissions and Exit in Focused Institutions

In this scenario, we are looking at a market for skills and competencies as the basis for a training, college and university system. Rather than focusing on open access and equity, here we are interested in developing skills and competencies through a process of progressive difficulty; moving on in a program of study or discipline is subject to ever increasing demands to demonstrate competency; only the "best learners" achieve distinction in their field. It is a kind of learner Darwinism.

For the majority of learners, whether in trades or college or university programs, this is the current system: only the very best high school students get into the very best schools and only those who graduate with honours and distinction go on to graduate study and of these a very small group get into doctoral programs and just over half of those who are admitted into such programs will complete. Both the US and the UK higher education systems were expanded on this premise in the 1960s. In the US, the widespread use of the SAT would identify working-class kids with high "scholastic aptitude"[41] and give them the academic chances they deserved. Need-based financial aid and government grants would ensure that everyone who wanted a college education could afford one. Affirmative action would diversify campuses and buoy disadvantaged minorities.

This is not, of course, how our current "system" describes itself. But this is the closest to how it works.

Let us look at one system in particular: Canada. Over the last several years, the grade point average of high school graduation (GPA) for admission to university has risen from 2.68 in 1990 to 2.94 in 2000 at the US's and Canada's elite universities[42]. In colleges, especially for programs in high demand (including high demand trades programs); a similar level of inflation can be seen. Indeed, one quality indicator often used by such institutions is the number of "qualified" candidates who they have turned away. It is ironic that many of the Professors who now teach in universities would not have secured admission as undergraduates if current admission requirements were applied.

In the US, money counts. In a 2005 review of meritocracy in The Atlantic, the author observes:

> "If you hope to obtain a bachelor's degree by age twenty-four, your chances are roughly one in two if you come from a family with an annual income over $90,000; roughly one in four if your family's income falls between $61,000 and $90,000; and slightly better than one in ten if it is between $35,000 and $61,000. For high-schoolers whose families make less than $35,000 a year the chances are around one in seventeen."[43]

What this competitive process does is place institutions in the driving seat of both what it is that learners learn and who it is they will permit to be learners. Rather than being an instrument of equity, such a system over time could become an instrument of inequity – one which marginalizes the abled, in favour of the very gifted (in talent and finances).

If such a system worked, then this would be an acceptable trade off given certain political philosophies. Indeed, a whole language was developed to describe "the rise of the meritocracy" to provide a rationale for socialists to sanction such selection on the basis of merit. It is, however, generally acknowledged that a pure meritocracy is probably impossible to achieve. What is less generally acknowledged is that such a system may not be entirely desirable. The limits and dangers of a system operating purely on the basis of merit were dramatically portrayed in *The Rise of the Meritocracy* (1961), a novel by British sociologist Michael Young. Young envisioned a society in which those at the top of the system ruled autocratically with a sense of righteous entitlement while those at the bottom of the system were incapable of protecting themselves against the abuses leveled against them from the merit elite above. Instead of a fair and enlightened society, the meritocracy became cruel and ruthless[44].

Another challenge to the idea of meritocracy is the level of dropout that occurs. The following chart, based entirely on Statistics Canada data, shows that choosing on the basis of demonstrated input competencies or assessment does not always lead to success for many learners. Taking the 2005 cohort admitted to all forms of program beyond school that involve accreditation (that is, it excludes non-credit continuing education and life-long learning activities), Statistics

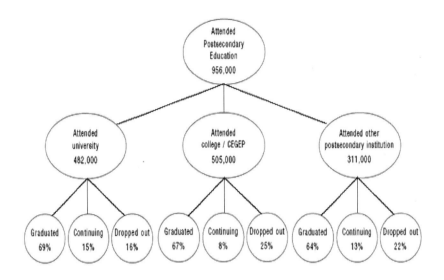

Canada looked at drop-out rates 6 years later. This is what they found: of the 956,000 learners registered, some 271,980 (28%) did not complete. Put simply: selection solely on the basis of merit is not a condition that leads to success for *all*. Of course, many drop out for a large range of reasons from personal circumstances, illness, financial hardship, family, work opportunities and so on. It is also the case that many who did drop out did obtain benefit from their learning. The point here is that competency based competitive admission has a significant down-side which is often not rationally discussed.

Apprenticeship is especially a thorny problem. Completion rates from apprenticeship programs vary considerably by program and by region. But they are low: 51% in Canada, for example, with very high drop-out for some trades (steam-fitter, industrial electrician, carpenter, for example)[45]. Part of the reason for this is the requirement that apprentices be employed for a key part of the apprenticeship and that they be supervised, coached and mentored by an accredited tradesman so as to obtain their "ticket". With economic change comes unemployment, restricting and accelerated retirement, which can have a direct impact on the apprentice – they lose their job, their mentor retires or loses his or her job and this disrupts their learning pathway.

The key characteristics of this scenario are:

1. Learners are "admitted" to programs of study at institutions on the basis of demonstrated competency and skills.
2. As learners progress through their education, fewer and fewer learners meet the competency and skills criteria for admission. The system involves a selection "funnel".
3. The primary drivers for this approach are: physical capacity (space as the final frontier); "quality" assumptions about learner: staff ratios (for example, how many PhD students can be supervised by one person); assumptions that the more demanding admission requirements will lead to a commensurately higher quality of learning; and ease of administration – the higher the skill set the less remediation is required.
4. There are also financial drivers – selection by merit is a form of resource rationing from a decreasing pot.

What this has given rise to are different tiers of institutions. In Alberta, Canada, for example, there are six tiers of post-secondary institutions in what is known as "Campus Alberta":

- **Comprehensive Academic and Research Institutions** – there are four fully functioning research driven universities in Alberta for a population of 3.7 million.
- **Baccalaureate and Applied Studies Institutions** – there are two "teaching" universities with only a modest research agenda at this time.
- **Polytechnic Institutions** – there are two Polytechnics offering programs from trade tickets to applied baccalaureate degrees.
- **Comprehensive Community Institutions** – there are eleven community colleges distributed throughout the

Province, each providing college services with some also offering applied degrees and baccalaureate degrees in partnerships with level 1 and 2 institutions.

- **Independent Academic Institutions** – there are five degree granting institutions which can be non-profit or for-profit offering baccalaureate and, in some cases, Masters degrees.
- **Specialized Arts and Culture Institutions** – there are two specialized institutions (the Banff Centre and the Alberta College of Art and Design) which are able to offer specialized degrees from baccalaureate level to PhD.

This is a total of twenty six institutions for a total population of 3.8 million. Ontario has some 24 universities and 20 community colleges for a population of some 10 million. Canada has in total 72 universities and 115 community colleges for a population of 32 million.

Here we see meritocracy as a structural-economic and political phenomenon. Second tier universities were established to deal with the fact that a large number of learners were not able to secure places in Tier One institutions; applied degrees in colleges were in part a response to this same challenge but also a response to employers wanting more "hands on" and practical skills. From a system perspective, there appears to be a plethora of choice but, in fact, the differences between institutions are more about "brand" and credibility than about anything else.

Complex post-secondary systems like those in Ontario and Alberta give rise to a variety of issues for this type of Merit-based scenario, including these:

- **The nature of brand and institutional differentiation** - what is it that differentiates one institution from another, other than location?
- **Costs** – can institutions compete on price as well as brand? Given the insistence of quality assurance regimes and collective agreements on certain common rules (especially

ratio of full-time to part-time faculty, faculty workloads, residency), many of the cost drivers that determine the price to students are the same across the system (Ontario, for example, has a single collective agreement for all colleges), reducing the scope for price based competition.

- **Transferability** – how transferable are credits obtained in one part of the system to another part of the system – from, say Tier 2 universities or Tier 3 colleges, to Tier 1 universities?
- **Faculty** – given the hierarchy of the systems created by jurisdictions, are faculty across the institutions to be seen as basically equivalent to one another or are they different? Is a political science faculty team at a research university "better than" (from the learners' point of view) to a political science faculty team at a teaching university or a community college, given that degrees in political science may be available at all three kinds of institutions?

Scenario 4: The Elite Institution Known for its Brand Position

This is the "ideal" model in the minds of some – institutions with a global reputation for being both difficult to get into (merit based selection); difficult to get through (demanding teaching and learning based on challenge and intensive instruction); and outstanding in terms of outcomes. Such institutions, it is said, will attract "the best" faculty and the most outstanding talent for *all* of the work that institution wishes to do. Whether it is a trades school seeking to produce the world's best practical nurses or plumbers or a university seeking to produce the best scholars in the disciplines it teaches, the key idea is that of the best qualified students working with the best qualified faculty on work driven by the faculty's own research and experience.

The key characteristic of this scenario revolves around the power of the faculty to determine what a program of study is, who should teach, who should be admitted to learn, how the learners should be assessed and evaluated and what supports learners should be given. The faculty "run the show". Well, to some extent. Ability to pay truly determines who gets admitted.

Fareed Zakaria of *Time Magazine* and CNN makes this observation[46]:

> "There are broad changes taking place at American universities that are moving them away from an emphasis on merit and achievement and toward offering a privileged experience for an already privileged group. State universities – once the highways of advancement for the middle class – have been utterly transformed in recent decades, under the pressure of rising costs and falling government support. A new book, *Paying for the Party: How College Maintains Inequality,* shows how many state schools have established a "party pathway," admitting more and more rich out-of-state kids who can afford hefty tuition bills but who are middling students."

- making the point that elitism based on the ability to pay is growing in the US and other jurisdictions which have reduced public support for post-secondary education. Elitism is rife. Zakaria concludes his remarks with this observation:

> "The most troubling trend in America in recent years has been the decline in economic mobility. The institutions that have been the best at opening access in the US have been its colleges and universities. If they are not working to reward merit, America will lose the dynamism that has long made it so distinctive."[47]

Also key to this scenario is the ideal of "academic freedom"- a much debased term which traditionally recognized that faculty parameters had a right to teach and speak to issues they chose and in a manner of their choosing. As a concept it has been "corrupted" to mean a variety of things, but at its heart it is a "freedom of expression" construct. In this scenario, such freedoms are paramount.

This academic freedom also determines the right of the institution to set standards and to define "quality". While there is an acceptance of a set of quality standards and protocols, for example (such as those provided by Provincial or Regional accrediting bodies), each institution's jealousy guards its own processes of self-determination and independence.

This model has traditionally been a description of a handful of university institutions, though many have now "cloned" the philosophy, language, and processes of such institutions and claimed that they apply to them. For example, in Britain many of the current "new" universities that used to be colleges or Polytechnics claim the same values and position as Oxford or Cambridge, despite the fact that doing so is largely inappropriate. The University of Cheshire is *not* Oxford or indeed anything like it. The University of Calgary isn't either.

Scenarios: Predicting Future Movements

We can look at current and future developments in terms of a shift in movement between the four scenarios we just described. That is, where the intentional and strategic actions of an organization or institution lead it to shift or be shifting from one position to another.

Brand Positioning

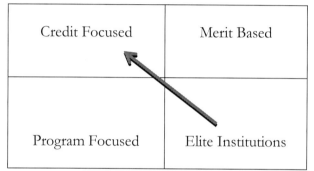

Move 1: From Elite to Credit Focused? Not Really!

Elite Universities, concerned about the perception of them becoming increasingly elite and unattainable, are pursuing practices which appear to place them in a more open and student centric position.

Harvard and MIT in the US and the Universities of Toronto and British Columbia in Canada, for example, are collaborating in offering MOOCs – elite universities seemingly pursuing open learning in partnership with the private sector. But in fact they are not. What they and others like them are doing is marketing and branding. They are "showcasing" their wares and making freely available to anyone these showcase courses so as to promote their brand. True openness would involve a systematic approach to advising with respect to learning pathways and a systematic approach to converting free to learn courses to credit. None of these institutions are pursuing these avenues at this time.

Their strategic intention is to attract more foreign students who better understand how the institution thinks about certain key subjects and embraces technology for learning. Rather than seeking to transform the "system", the elite institutions are leveraging technology to market and position themselves as brand leaders and demonstrating this in new ways to a growingly technologically savvy market.

Less Open, More Elite

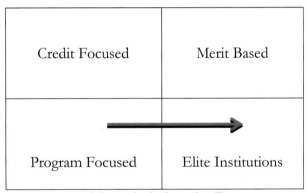

Credit Focused	Merit Based
Program Focused	Elite Institutions

Move 2: Aping the Best

In part because the elite universities "set the gold standard" for the "market and the market rules", less well known institutions which began with good intentions (openness, willingness to support remedial programs, creative approaches to programming, eschewing degrees in favour of community driven and employer needed programs) have started to ape the work of the elite universities.

The classic example is Britain: In the Harold Wilson government of 1964, a strong commitment was made to access to a new kind of post-secondary institution – the Polytechnic. The purpose of the poly was to offer on the same campus programs in demand from the workplace – short courses, apprenticeship, professional development – together with a range of community driven programs, degrees, diplomas and certificates. Academic degrees in polytechnics were validated by the UK Council for National Academic Awards (CNAA) from 1965 to 1992. The CNAA was chartered by the British government to award degrees and maintain national quality assurance standards. The CNAA subject boards from their inception were from the universities. Over time, the Polytechnics used degrees to boost revenues and increase enrollment and gradually lost their broader purpose.

By 1992, the Polytechnics were all but universities – they had cloned the University model – and this was recognized in the UK's *Further and Higher Education Act*. Lancashire Polytechnic became the University of Central Lancashire and all thirty four Polytechnics of the United Kingdom are now universities. By this process, a major engine of innovation in post-secondary education in Britain was dimmed if not lost.

From Merit to Elite

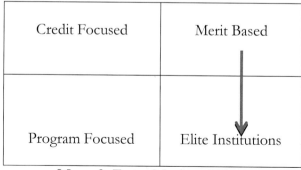

Credit Focused	Merit Based
Program Focused	Elite Institutions

Move 3: From Merit to Elite

The decline of meritocracy and the lowering of mobility of the middle class have led to a shift in the admission strategies of some (but not all) colleges and universities to a more elitist view of their role. We have already described this and cited some evidence to suggest that this is occurring, at least in the UK and the US.

The problem with this view, even though we can see it is occurring, is that it misunderstands why this is occurring. There are several reasons, including these:

- When a public education system is privatized by stealth – one interpretation of the substantial cut in public funding for training, colleges and universities – then institutions will seek to secure guaranteed payments from those most able to pay. The most able to pay may not be those who can benefit most from the education available. They start to game the system, as is already occurring in GERM based K-12 systems[48].
- The growth of international students is also a reflection of the fact that they pay substantially higher fees and that there are growing numbers of them. China alone graduates some seven million a year, many of whom go on to seek graduate programs abroad.
- Because of the proliferation of degree granting institutions (most community colleges can now offer applied degrees or baccalaureate degrees); established universities are able to "cream" from the applicant pool's more able and more able to pay applicants.
- Able students are thus no longer able to secure the grades that were once acceptable – admission grade inflation excludes them. So they seek to secure places at their third, fourth, fifth or sixth choices.

The reality here is that the "elite" generally stay elite for a considerable time (though international comparisons do show the steady rise of some institutions). Breaking in to the truly elite category is difficult to do.

Program Focus to Credit Focus

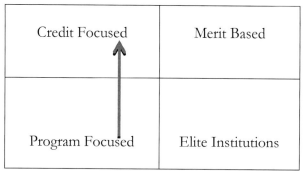

Move 4: From Programs to Credit

This shift occurs when an institution which has been a program focused, student centered and generally open institution, expands its services to move to competency based and outcomes based assessment irrespective of where the learner obtained that learning. That is, they significantly expand their prior learning assessment and recognition (PLAR) and work-based learning services at the expense of their traditional course and program offerings.

This is not often or currently seen in the post-secondary institutional space, but can be seen in the professional learning organizations (accounting and engineering certification, for example) where professional bodies have shifted from offering their own programs and courses to providing competency based and transfer credit (PLAR based) or challenge assessments for individuals.

This is also a trend which is supported by the growing number of international agreements with respect to learner mobility (e.g. the Commonwealth Small Countries Transnational Framework and the

Bologna Accord) and is a "designed in" feature of the EU's strategy for lifelong learning by 2020.

Conclusion

Using some scenario mapping and modeling, we outline some ways of looking at current developments in the higher education. We do so because this provides a way of conceptualization patterns and strategic trends rather than reacting to tactical or local developments.

Seven Key Considerations for Decision Makers

The scenarios presented here can help to clear the "fog" that has so many decision makers (quite rightly) paralyzed in their thinking, not knowing how to respond when things are in flux in these 'in between times'.

It can also seem like post-secondary education has been forgotten about in the face of that more hard-hitting crisis in our healthcare systems and economy. Many mid-level decision makers may feel out on their own, unsure about which direction to move in. Not being in the spotlight is actually a great position to be in. It enables experimentation and can provide the opportunity to affect some real change. For those in a decision making position we offer some critical considerations to crystallize strategic direction and the related decisions that need to be made. We suggest that it is important first to "map" the moves that institutions are making in terms of the scenarios we have just outlined, and then explore these seven issues from a strategic policy and operational perspective.

1. Quality

It's about 'fit for purpose', not 'fit for league tables'

Many jurisdictions have struggled with the definition of quality in higher education when applying it to a process of educating minds rather than the building of widgets. Currently, quality in higher education has veered towards being defined by league tables based on reputation, research dollars and peer reviewed articles and business processes- ultimately inhibiting innovation.

There is a need to shift from an input-output and process framework for quality to a framework that is based on the 'fitness for purpose' from the learner point of view. This quality framework moves us away from the measurement of what doesn't matter for the educational process and gets back to the essence of what an education is for: the need or desire to learn and secure a great experience of learning - whether or not the *purpose* of that learning is to upgrade basic skills, to remain relevant in the job market, to perfect a technology or to expand one's horizons. A focus on engagement, interactions, mastery of competency, service and experience would start to provide a basis of change in which the learner would feel that they could have an impact both on their own experience and that of others.

What could a quality learning environment look like? It should focus on student recruitment and retention, student engagement and service quality, instructor engagement and satisfaction and the culture of the organization.

More specifically, we should ask these questions:

- Who secures access to learning and on what basis?
- How aligned are the "arrival" assumptions of learners with their actual experience of the institution?
- Who is retained and what are the primary reasons for student drop-out? What actions is the institution taking to significantly increase retention, satisfaction and completion rates?
- What are the failure rates in each course? For courses with high failure rates, what is being done to redesign the learning experience and what plans are there to secure high completion rates in these courses in the future?
- What competencies do learner assessments during the career of a learner assess and how? What is the process and experience of continuous improvement of assessment?
- What do measures of student engagement indicate about the extent to which they are engaged in their learning, with their instructors, with learner peers, with learning materials and with their chosen industry or profession?
- What are the indicators of student service (turnaround times, service standard compliance, etc.)? What complaints have

been made by students or instructors and what response has there been to these complaints?

- How extensively are remediation and support services used by learners and what could be done to improve their utilization and value?
- What are the indicators of instructor satisfaction showing?
- How engaged are instructors with their students learning challenges?
- What investments in professional development and capacity building for improved student engagement, learning design, e-learning and blended learning are being made and what impact are they having on the performance of learners?
- What is the quality of strategic and operational leadership in the organization?
- Is there a service and student engagement culture in the organization?
- When third parties look at the institution from a service perspective (employers for example), what feedback do they provide about the experience of working with the institution and its learners and graduates?
- What third party accreditation and certification has the institution received?
- Are the business and academic planning processes of the institution IS9001 certified?

These are not the questions currently providing the basis of quality assurance in QA systems adopted nationally or internationally. But these are the quality questions a "fitness for purpose" focused system would address.

2. Flexibility, Access & Choice

It's about the working learner, from overseas, as well the high-schooler

This challenge is driven by demographics... what the demographic data is saying is that the working learner is on the rise and that they are demanding different things than the high-schoolers. No longer is the typical learner straight from high school who is ready to take their one diploma or degree before embarking on a career. In fact, this demographic is on the decline. Many coming into post-secondary learning are taking the "scenic route" via work or periodically returning to learning while working or alternating between work and learning. Indeed, our colleague, Professor Jón Torfi Jónasson of the School of Education University of Iceland suggested that we might represent the shift from an old paradigm of the connection between education and work and the new visually as follows:

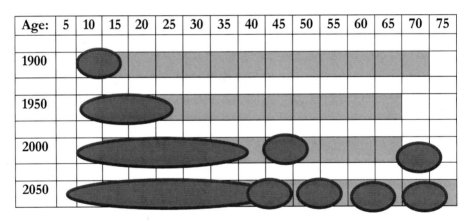

Periods of Education Represented by shaded bubble
Periods of Work Represented by the Shaded Area

This shows repeated period of learning either while in work or between periods of work gradually growing since 1950 and the period of compulsory education and needed education expanding. By 2050, between 70 and 75% of the workforce will need a post-secondary education for employment and continuing and life-long education to be able to maintain employment.

This student demographic is demanding flexibility in the delivery of programs and access to a choice of programs, not necessarily from just one institution and not necessarily from within their own jurisdiction. They are also demanding greater flexibility in credit granting and transferability. For the majority of learners, the place of delivery is not a factor, (unless you can get into an elite institution); it is about what the learning can do for them in achieving their learning personal goals.

With immigration being a big issue for the post-industrializing nations who are struggling to maintain growth and attract the brightest minds, flexibility and access plays "big" into this. The demand isn't for e-learning -it is for flexibility. There needs to be flexibility in the way in which we recognize education and award qualifications. Business as usual is no longer viable in the medium to long term. This is why we envisage the growth of credit granting institutions who act independently of the provision of learning.

3. User Pay vs. Public Funds

It's about paying attention to whom now actually pays.

Postwar years were a boon for the public investment in higher education - funds were plentiful for those few higher education institutions that existed. As the push to expand higher education for all (mainly the baby boomers) grew and the number of institutions bloomed, the fiscal realities of funding public education started to hit home. In the 1980s and 90s, students and their families were increasingly asked to pay a larger share of an education. Governments were backing away from equity as a driver and funding their systems around meritocratic principles (they thought).

Across Canada, the proportion of the costs of the higher education that students were asked to pay gradually increased and now hover around a one-third/two thirds split with government. In Alberta, a tuition freeze in 2010 meant that student fees as a proportion of costs officially continues to hover around this level, but signs say that this could be creeping around to the 50% level. It is a new form of public:private individual partnership (we might refer to it as a PiP), but the governance and control regulations still generally assume that higher education is a public good and that the decisions made between governments and institutions count for more than the legally binding service agreements between students and the institution.

Where universities get their money (as % of total operating revenue)		
Year	Government funding	Tuition fees
1977	84.0%	13.7%
1987	81.4%	16.3%
1997	67.1%	29.0%
2007	57.1%	34.2%

Source: Statistics Canada and CAUBO[49]

The question we ask here is simple: At what point does the accountability shift? When do the students secure a larger role in governance and strategic decision making in return for their near equal investment with Government (who they also provide the funds for)?

It also behooves a smart legislator to shift its focus on enabling more students to individually bear their financial burden with supportive, smart financial mechanisms rather than dictating to an institution how, when and where it spends its government funds. They may also need to shift their focus to student and consumer protection.

4. Partnerships for Teaching and Learning

It's about teaching in collaboration, in and outside the academe.

A hallmark of the GERM approach to post-secondary education is to use markets and competition to determine "quality" – those constantly in high demand and with high streams of revenue from market activities "win" while those who don't game the system but seek to provide equitable access and meaningful education to all who seek to enter are more likely to be deemed losers.

A characteristic of effective use of public and private (including individual) resources is collaboration. That is, collaboration between institutions; between institutions and employers; between institutions and community organizations and non profits; and between individuals and programs within the organization. For example, collaborative degrees or diplomas, such as that between the Moscow Power Engineering Institute (a technical university) and the Technical University of Lappeenranta (Finland). Russian MPEI students participating in this program are trained in joint Master of Science course in the streams Electrical Engineering, Power Electrical Engineering and Bioengineering and, on completion, obtain two diplomas after graduation in the joint program (one from each institution). These students are trained partially in Moscow and partially in Finland - the education is organized in English. This is an example of one of much such collaboration between Finland and other institutions. Brazil has developed an exchange program, similar to that between Russia and Finland. To date, this program has involved 36 students each year and has achieved these six outcomes:

1. Provide students with the language, culture, technical, and business skills to work for international companies;
2. Create course articulation agreements for transferring of credits between participating institutions;
3. Develop a system for linguistic and cultural preparation for students participating in the foreign exchange;

4. Provide industry with culturally and technically proficient professionals qualified to work in several locations for multi-national companies;
5. Document results of successful relationships between program participants (students, institution administration, participating faculty, industry advisory committee) that lead to educational and disciplinary research;
6. Develop outreach activities to make the program better known inside and outside the consortium. These activities include: development of program website, publishing and presenting conference papers, giving talks at both the home and host institutions.

Such international partnerships enrich student learning, prepare graduates to work in multi-national organizations and can accelerate learning completions when such partnerships permit year round learning.

There are other kinds of collaboration which are also very effective. In Australia, since 1993, a group of universities have collaborated in the founding of a for profit co-operative enterprise known as Open Universities Australia (OUA)[50]. It now offers 1700 units and 180 qualifications online- all taught by 20 leading universities and other tertiary education providers around Australia. Students chose which of the key providers they wish to obtain their qualification from. It offers undergraduate and graduate programs and does so through Asia as well as Australia. In 2012, it served 60,000 students from 89 countries and returned a profit in excess of AUS$20million on revenues of AUS$191 million.

Middlesex University in the UK has pioneered work-based learning accreditation in the UK. In this kind of collaboration, employers offering significant professional and technical education to their own staff can also be assured that employees who successfully complete these in-house programs can be awarded credit for diploma, bachelor's, master's and doctoral degrees – with the bulk of these degrees and diplomas being earned in this way. For many years, for example, *Marks and Spenser* (a major UK retailer) could provide a route to a Bachelors or Masters degree through their world-leading in house training. Similar arrangements are now available at other UK universities[51].

While many colleges and universities have been engaged in co-op education, their need to control teaching and credit granting has inhibited transformative use of these kinds of programs. By increasing the use of prior learning assessment and recognition (PLAR) and Work Based Learning (WBL), shifting to a competency and outcome based approach to learning rather than a time-served and process approach, major collaborative opportunities for learning in the workplace or community can be created.

Policy makers need to remove any barriers to such developments, such as current regulations governing credit hours and credit granting, residency and the use of the Carnegie unit as a way of assessing the financial incentives for institutions to admit students, design programs and grant credit. Shifting to an outcome based post-secondary system would foster such a collaborative approach and help to improve productivity and performance of the system as a whole.

5. Changing Nature of Technology and Business Models

It's about thinking of investing in engaging pedagogy rather than just more bricks and mortar.

There is one more thing certain in life than death and taxes: by the time you have invested in a technology, a new technology development will have occurred that significantly reduces the value of the investment made. The only thing that uncertain is how fast that change will happen, but it's well known that where as some breakthroughs in technological advancement actually occur within an institution it's increasingly just as likely, if not more likely to happen faster in the workplace or private company. This is because:

1. Private companies -they make technology investment decisions which focus on keeping up to date with latest technology so as to improve productivity, performance and business process.
2. Private companies do not see buildings and new infrastructure as attractive – indeed many are opting to get out of the buildings business and lease them back (through REITs) – what they see as attractive is a constant focus on performance and outcomes – technology helps.
3. They are not hindered by inhibiting collective agreements which impair their ability to leverage technology to change how core activities are done.
4. They want constantly to increase the scale and scope of their market reach.
5. They are willing to take strategic risks so as to stay current and cutting edge and keep pushing the boundaries of discovery.

We have said that technology is a distraction, but only at the cost of thinking it's the panacea for the system. It isn't, but neither is building more expensive buildings or hiring more and more faculty members. Focused investments in key technologies linked to changes in the business models for the design, development, deployment and delivery of learning are.

The key is that technology and new business models together permit institutions to achieve scale – increase affordable access and quality at the same time.

6. Tenure and Faculty

It's about incentivizing the faculty to be innovative.

Organizations will tend to favour decision making towards the dominant voice at the table. By far, the dominant voice at any decision making body in a post-secondary institution is the faculty. It is not always appropriate that they are.

Tenure (seniority in the college system) is currently a very sensitive labour issue within the post-secondary system. In the university sector, it's essentially seen as a system which confers a job for life to an academic until they chose to retire or the institution runs out of money.

Tenure is a relatively recent introduction considering the history of the academy and was created to protect academic freedom after a series of late 19th-century incidents when university donors, politicians and legislators tried to remove professors whose views they disliked. The protection of academic freedom is still a valid concern and can be protected by means other than tenure.

However, in April 2009, *Washington Post* article[52] by Francis Fukuyama, who served as a tenured economics professor at Johns Hopkins University, demonstrated that even a growing number of professors want to abolish tenure. Fukuyama said that not only is tenure a financial burden on universities, but it also "hamstrings younger untenured professors, making them fearful of taking intellectual risks and causing them to write in jargon aimed only at those in their narrow sub-discipline".

Margaret Thatcher determined to abolish tenure in the UK university system and did so in 1998. Academic staff, with a few exceptions, are employed for contractual periods of time (5, 10, 15 or more years) with a performance based contract of employment. Promotion remains guided by the same rules as existed before tenure was abolished – quality of research and teaching and service to the community. The assumption the Thatcher administration made was that this move would make the institutions more nimble and responsive, would improve outcomes and remove from within the ranks of the Professoriate "dead wood" protected by tenure.

Tenure locks in big costs and makes it difficult for universities to explore more productive teaching techniques. Mark C. Taylor, chair of Columbia University's Department of Religion and author of a book critical of tenure, estimates that a college ties up between $10 million and $12 million of its endowment to support a single tenured professor for a 35-year career. A 2011 study of teaching practices at the University of Texas at Austin indicated that UT Austin alone potentially could save $266 million a year if it could get half its professors to be as productive in teaching as the top 20%, fire it's least productive faculty, and shift their small workload to other professors.

Tenure also limits how nimble colleges can be in deploying their staff to subject areas that will better equip students for employment or respond to community needs. As a 2010 study by the Center for College Affordability, a non-profit research center, expressed it: "With a tenure system, colleges are not able to reduce the number of medieval history professors in order to increase the number of information technology and business professors."

Academic teaching techniques remain calcified, despite a technological revolution in the last 20 years that enables professors to impart their knowledge in more effective and efficient ways. For example, a 2011 UCLA study of 6,768 US undergraduate male teachers of science, technology, engineering and math subjects (so-called STEM) found 70% still relied on lectures while only 33% used student inquiry-type methods or e-learning.

Every university and college's business school has taught how restrictive work practices and legacy commitments lead to high labour costs which, for many years, made many North American and EU industries less competitive. Now universities and colleges need to adopt their own teaching and end tenure.

7. The "TINA" Belief system- There Is No Alternative

It's about challenging the inertia to change, not keeping on doing what we've always been doing because we believe we can now get different results.

Inertia and atrophy is inherent in any system. Voices like "it's always been this way" and "there is nothing anyone can do" always exist, but paradigm shift and classic belief systems change - especially when there is overwhelming evidence to suggest a new perspective is needed and that the time for change is now.

We're seeing rapid disengagement from current education systems by the young people, due to the rapidly rising cost of education, a growing concern about the relevance and value of postsecondary education amongst the student and potential student body and employers. Young people are asking: "is it worth it?"

To borrow what our high school Physics teachers drummed into us about the Newton's first law of motion which describes an object's tendency to resist changes in their motion, i.e. the atoms or structures (read institutions) want to "keep on doing what they're doing". This is classic inertia and can be found in our complex economic and social systems as well as a tiny atom.

In January 2013, Moody's Investors Service put a negative outlook on the entire US higher education sector, even at major research universities, which had been spared in previous forecasts. And that came after a year in which the agency downgraded the credit ratings of 22 colleges, including Alabama A&M, Wellesley College and Morehouse College. At the same time, Standard & Poor's Ratings Service downgraded 13 institutions, including Amherst College, Tulane University and Yeshiva University. Combined, both agencies upgraded only eight colleges and universities in 2012. Only 500 or so of the 4,000-plus colleges and universities in the United States seem to have stable enough finances to be truly safe from bankruptcy. The remaining institutions, where a vast majority of Americans attend, can no longer hold off the technological, demographic and economic forces quickly bearing down on them. Just because we believe that colleges are a public trust and shouldn't fail doesn't mean they won't.

Across Canada and in the UK, college and university finances are similarly precarious – the business model is broken and, even though many of the UK and Canadian institutions are guaranteed through "public ownership" it does not mean that there will not be closures, mergers and acquisitions. One of the authors of this book's undergraduate university college no longer exists due to financial mismanagement. In Alberta, all four research universities are financially challenged. In Ontario, several colleges and universities are in tough financial positions. In every jurisdiction some institutions are thriving, but these mask the weakness of the model for those who are not.

So when the business model is clearly broken there are three choices: (a) wait and hope it gets better, relying on "handouts" and short term "fixes" to cushion the wait – the current strategy in most government, colleges and universities; (b) reinvent and re-imagine the business model so that the problem is tackled at its root – the strategy systematically avoided by universities, colleges and governments; or (c) cease operations. A few have chosen the latter and pursued mergers and acquisition so as to enable students to complete programs and the impact of the closure to be minimized. Few have ever pursued the reinvention or re-imagine route, though the world is already littered with alternatives to the dominant way of doing things[53].

The challenge, then, is clear: What should the future look like – what is the new business model? Our section on scenarios (see pages 50 - 79) provides some clues to the future. Our final section will build on these clues and the imperatives included in this section and suggest some approaches to rethinking post-secondary education.

The Three Big Enabling Opportunities for Change and Rethinking Post-Secondary Education

How do we make sense of the competing and sometimes distracting features of the current developments in higher education? How do we find a path through the maze of opportunity? In this closing section of the book we seek to provide a framework for responding to the need to change and the dynamics of the market place.

We begin by understanding some major lessons from the observations we have been making throughout this book and from our day to work with colleges, universities and private sector educators over the last decade. We suggest:

1.   **In the face of challenge, threat or change, our institutions will seek to constrain innovation from new entrants and third parties.**

The adoption of restrictive practices, market protection and related measures will be in response to perceived threats from private sector players, global players and new entrants from the public sector in other jurisdictions. The risk here is that in seeking to protect existing practices, the opportunities for real change and collaboration across borders and institutional boundaries will be lost. This would be a short-sighted response. We should learn from competition and thrive on the opportunity the competition provides to improve, change and develop new forms of institution, new pedagogy and new programs.

2.   **Leaders who try to change their institutions will be left out in the cold by their institutions.**

We have seen this in prestigious institutions like Oxford and elsewhere in the world. In fact, it is becoming increasingly difficult to recruit talented people to leadership roles from Deans upwards in colleges and universities. At the heart of the challenge for our future is the need for courageous, visionary leadership. We need to enable more courageous leaders, including from the student body, if our system is to thrive rather than just survive. Courage, vision and commitment will be key. We need renaissance leadership for our colleges and universities.

3. Faculty members will become highly mobile.

For years, colleges and universities have been warning of the coming implications of the grey tsunami. It is now beginning to occur. Faculty members who are skilled and highly effective teachers and researchers will be in high demand and will trade their skills for pay and time and move more frequently.

4. Universities and colleges will lag so far behind the emerging technologies for learning that students will vote with their feet and study with those institutions elsewhere in the world who "get with the technology".

Many institutions appear "unsure" of their strategy with respect to learning, technology and assessment and, in turn, lag behind in their adoption of emerging technologies. As technologies become cheaper and more powerful (Moore's law) and more ubiquitous, then this issue will become a determining factor in student choice. This will be enabled by transfer credit and prior learning assessment, especially if the "residency" requirement, usually that 50% of credits for a program awarded by an institution must be taken at that institution, changes. Imagine a program that has no residency requirements where credits can be obtained from anywhere in the world.

5. Maintaining government funding through the Carnegie unit, payment for fixed hours of study in a course, will inhibit innovation.

A major system constraint is the way in which institutions are funded. If the current model persists, then institutions will continue to offer the kind of programs and choices they offer now. To secure innovation, new funding models are required. Without these, the system may well atrophy. Those institutions which have shifted to outcome-based funding are seeing more innovation and higher levels of student registration such as the state of Kentucky with its on demand program.

6.   **Linear learning paths are not how students will learn in the 21st Century.**

Increasingly, students will stop and start, drop in and out of their learning. For them, learning is a personal journey and a life-long one. But institutions still think of cohorts, program completions and time to complete. By thinking of personalized learning pathways as the route by which students learn, institutions will change what they do. The risk is that many institutions will make this more difficult than it needs to be.

7.   **Institutions will price themselves out of some communities and some target groups.**

Costs are increasing from a student perspective – the costs of post-secondary education constitute a significant portion of Canadian household debt. At some point, we need to recognize the impact of this on a variety of groups and society and then re-think student support and financial aid.

8.   **First Nations students and the socially disadvantaged will feel increasingly marginalized in expensive systems which focus on forms of learning which are a-cultural and do not speak to their concerns.**

First Nations students are a fast growing cohort, yet their success in the post-secondary system is weak. More and more individuals are also falling into the group labeled "social disadvantage". Many of the directions in which the system is going are counter to their preferred way of learning and many new programs are "alien" to their understanding of need. We need to build new bridges and adaptive institutions to meet their needs.

9.   **The link between post-secondary education and the needs of the fast changing labour market will become more and more disconnected.**

We are preparing students in school, college and university for a world that is fast changing and for jobs and roles which are just emerging and are ill defined. We do so increasingly by competency / skills-based learning. Yet what we really need is life-long learners who have core skills and adaptive abilities who are intrapreneurs, entrepreneurs and resilient. Do we have the right forms of learning to enable this to occur?

This summary of key observations from our practice suggests to us that we need a strategic focus for change, otherwise we will be seduced by the distractions we described earlier.

Strategically Focused Change

Our beginning assumptions about a strategy for change are that it should focus on three key intentions:

1. Enabling Access and Equity
2. Enabling Structural Innovation
3. Enabling Pedagogic Innovation

1. Enabling Access and Equity

The key is to focus not on institutions but on the needs of learners. They are seeking flexibility, responsiveness and recognition driven by their personal and economic circumstances. We have mistaken this for a call for more capital expansion to permit more institutional capacity, an expansion of e-learning or new approaches to co-operative education. These are all institutionally focused solutions which reinforce a growing fragile business model of post-secondary education. What we need is a rethink of the system from a learner perspective.

So as to meet the demand for **flexibility and access**, post-secondary systems should:

- **Move to an outcome based funding of the system.** Organizations are rewarded in terms of achieving a range of outcomes. In policy terms, this is "block grant funding with outcome expectations" – moving from "line item accountability" to results based management and ending the reliance on the Carnegie unit.
- **Move to a focus on competency based credit recognition.** Rather than seeing credit as a reward for time-served and assessment completion, see credit as a statement of competency. Credit is awarded to a learner who can demonstrate competency irrespective of how they obtained the knowledge, understanding and skills required to do so. This permits the separation of credit recognition from the process of instruction – something that would be a major breakthrough for learners.
- **Create new Provincial, State or National organizations to undertake competency assessment, prior learning assessment and enter into work-based learning agreements leading to credit recognition.** The American Council on Education and many professional bodies have done this. For example, The National Institute for the Uniform Licensing of Power Engineers (NIULPE) was conceived in 1972 as an organization which promotes and formalizes measures designed to advance safety in all matters related to the management of energy. It was incorporated in 1972 as a not-for-profit organization and third-party certification organization that acts on an international level to establish standards for the education, safety and assessment of the

power engineering and related industry. It sets assessments and provides competency based recognition.

- **Abolish residency requirements.** A true barrier to productivity and access is the requirement, claimed to be a quality requirement (but is in fact largely a financial matter), that 50% or more of a credential should be "earned" at the institution providing a credential. A truly innovative and creative system focused on access, equity and productivity would see this requirement as a barrier and work to remove it.

- **Ensure transferability of learning and competencies.** A student who has mastered a body of knowledge or a skill and has been recognized for doing so through the award of credit should not have to repeat this learning. Transfer should not be optional, subject to conditional review by an individual instructor, but should be mandated and required. It should be seen as a student right.

- **Break down courses into competency based modules.** We have checked all of the scriptures for many religions and cannot find a commandment that says that courses bearing credit should generally be 13-15 weeks long and worth 3 credits. Courses should be the length required to master a competency or skill or a specific body of knowledge. Some courses will still be worth 3 credits. But courses could also be weighted as .25, .33, .5 or 1 credit. Following the lead of the Kentucky Community and Technical College System (KCTCS)[54], modular based credit which can be accumulated for transfer should be the norm, not the exception.

- **End the semester as a start and end point for learning.** Modules and learning activities should be available for start 365 days of the year, with modules ending at a time appropriate for the credit weighting. For example, a .25 module might be 3 weeks while a .33 module four weeks. This requires a rethink of the business model of institution and the system of learner support. The majority of students in colleges and universities are now adult learners not the "traditional" high-schooler – they require this flexibility, as several studies have shown[55].

- **Offer MOOCs with credit assessment for the "gateway" courses.** Gateway courses are those which are required for transfer from community college to university or are the foundation courses for college certificates, diplomas and apprenticeships. If all of these courses were MOOCs free to learners to undertake anytime, anywhere and credit was available through proctored challenge examinations or other forms of competency based credit assessment, then access and equity would be addressed directly and significant new capacity would be built in the system by design. Further, "master courses" – world-leading versions of these courses – could create real significant jurisdictional advantage and global recognition for the first jurisdiction to pursue this.

- **Stimulate collaborative program offerings**. If students can chose a home institution, but be able to complete modules from anywhere or secure credit through challenge or prior learning assessment because there are no residency restrictions and if credit is based on competency not time served then the business model changes. If this is coupled with outcome based funding rather than the Carnegie unit as the basis of institutional support, this should foster the collaborative development of competency based modules by colleges and universities working together. The key barrier to this is, at this time, the financial reward system for institutions and the way in which competition rather than collaboration is fostered by the pursuit of outmoded quality and accountability rubrics within the GERM framework for post-secondary education systems.

- **Rethink pedagogy and the role of instructors (faculty).** The majority of faculty members still practice "chalk and talk", though blended learning is gaining ground. What a rethought postsecondary system will need is a new approach to pedagogy which gives support to the flipped classroom, flexible and modular learning and 365 start dates for learners. To enable this, new contracts of employment will be needed and fundamental changes in pedagogy must drive these contracts. This pedagogical focus should emphasize the coaching, guiding and mentoring functions of faculty, the need for learner engagement and project based and mindful learning versus the mastery of knowledge required for assessments. Tenure has no place in a new contract.

- **Rethink student financing.** Cash flows to institutions will be very different under the approach outlined here – rather than per capita funding, institutions would be funded by block grants based on agreed outcomes. If time in class is no longer the basis of funding institutions, it should no longer be the basis of funding students through scholarships, loans and bursaries. While some countries (Scotland and Finland, for example) provide free postsecondary education for their citizens (thereby ensuring equitable access), outcome based financing for learners needs now to be looked at. Payment of the minimum wage pro-rated by learner commitments and outcome based performance measures may be a model worth exploring. The driver for this re-imagined system of student finance has to be equity + commitment = outcomes.

- **Significantly expand student support services.** Students need a concierge service for advising (learning advice, study skills, careers, financial) and support (help desk support, navigating course choice). They also need service agreements and an Ombudsman. While many of these services are provided at an institutional level, they may be better provided at a State, Provincial or National level. Flexible options and choice require dedicated professional support.

These twelve changes would radically transform postsecondary education and lead such systems to be student and outcome focused, not institution and faculty focused. In terms of our scenarios, a move from meritocratic and elite systems to credit granting and student program focused systems. But they are not, on their own, enough. Structural innovation is also needed.

2. Enabling Structural Innovation

Higher education systems have become complex, labrynthian and adept at contrapreneurship. There is a need for significant structural transformation. This should be driven not by a desire to appease existing institutional interests, but from a focus on learners, equity and performance. Transformation requires a commitment to significant change and a willingness to stare down the vested interests of faculty, administrators and some organizations that see change as an anathema to their understanding of governance.

Higher education institutions should be focused on making learning accessible, affordable, engaging, effective and meaningful for their learners. They should be constantly striving to improve completion rates, deliver student driven quality learning and enable effective pedagogy to be practiced by investing in the development of pedagogic capacity. They should also be fiscally accountable and transparent – results based management should be the heart of management and administrative practice. Their role is not to protect faculty or administration, but to respond creatively, flexibly and efficiently to changing student and community needs.

Here are our suggestions as to how this can be achieved:

- **Federated Governance.** In Alberta there are six universities for a population of 3.8 million people. Each has their own infrastructure, governance and financial and human resource operations. It makes no sense. There should be a single governance and "back office" function for all – the federated university model. The same should apply to the college / polytechnic sector – rather than there being twelve colleges and two polytechnics, Alberta should have a Community and Technical College system along the lines of the Kentucky system. Not only would this produce economies of scale, it would enable real innovation, reduction of duplication and system rationalization. Federated governance is a significant opportunity missed in most jurisdictions.
- **Invest in leadership capacity building.** Vice Chancellors and Presidents, Provosts and Vice Presidents and Deans receive little (if any) training for their difficult roles. Most have no business background, for example, but are responsible for multi-million dollar operations, significant human resource challenges and performance management and accountability systems as well as fundraising, public relations and capital infrastructure. We need to enhance the capacity of institutional leaders to lead in changing times.
- **Fund by outcomes not per capita/time.** Ending the funding of institutions by the Carnegie unit and provide block grants to achieve social, educational and knowledge (research) outcomes against an agreed results based business plan. For $X we will achieve Y. Hold the institution accountable for what they say they will do and provide incentives for the achievement of desirable learning and social outcomes.
- **Don't mix funds for learning with funds for research.** Universities and many colleges and polytechnics claim that research is the key driver for the knowledge based economy and, at a very general level, they are right.

Governments, however, confuse this claim with the idea that research should be applied and lead to commercialization. This is generally not what universities do well (if at all), though colleges and polytechnics are beginning to show promise. Support basic research. See applied research and commercialization as something not core to the work of colleges or universities but something which they can contribute to. Develop independent, applied and commercial research institutes with clear strategic intentions, focused programmes of work and seconded staff – problem solving centres which do exactly that and, when done, the program ends. Such organizations exist - Fraunhofer-Gessellschaft Society (Germany), The Whitehead Institute for Biomedical Research (Cambridge, Massachusetts) and SRI International (Menlo Park, California) are examples – and should be linked to a focused effort to build jurisdictional advantage.

- **Separate learning as a process from credit recognition**. By all means, let universities and colleges award credit, but do not see these as having an exclusive right to do so. Create a stand-alone, collaborative agency that uses all of the available means to recognize learning through competency based assessments.

- **Enable year round, 365 start dates**. So as to increase access, flexibility and appropriateness, modularize courses so that students can accumulate their learning credits starting whenever they are ready.

- **Require transferability of credit and end residency**. Competency based credits and other credits should be transferable to any institution at any time. Learner mobility is a critical factor in labour mobility and barriers to such learner mobility should be removed. Some jurisdictions have used the power of statute to enforce transfer; others have simply made it a condition of State or provincial funding. Waiting for a voluntary system of transfer, as we can see in many jurisdictions, does not work. Force the issue. As for residency, this is also a barrier to learner mobility.

- **Redesign the quality assurance regime**. Throughout this book we have challenged the model of quality assurance in use by existing quality assurance regimes. It's time to change the focus of this away from "institutional protection" and towards student focused quality. Some aspects of the present system can be retained (e.g. requirements for institutional capacity and sustainability), but others should be replaced by a strong focus on the student experience, engagement, service and culture.
- **Require collaboration and discourage competition**. Jurisdictions that hold equity as the underlying value need to end the idea that institutions compete and enable and require collaboration. Federated governance is part of this process, but so too is the notion of a changed business model. Rather than competing for students, since this is how funds are allocated, remove this element of competition by changing the funding model and focus on quality (redefined), flexibility and results-based management to achieve outstanding results.
- **Support the growth of public : private partnerships**. Increasingly, private sector organizations play a key part in learning over the life-time of a learner. Colleges and universities should find partnerships and alliances that recognize this and make much more extensive use of work-based learning for credit, co-operative programs and systematic approaches to international education through placements and projects.
- **Enable the growth of the private sector in higher education**. Henley Management College, before it obtained its Royal Charter in 1991, provided education at the Masters level in business and recommended its successful learners for degrees to Brunel University, who had agreed to accept these "as presented", since Brunel

accepted that HMC knew what it was doing – it was one of the few business schools in the world to achieve triple accreditation from three different accrediting bodies[56]. This kind of partnership – growingly common in the UK and Europe – needs now to be extended. We should encourage creative experimentation with program offering and partnership so as to expand access, reach and enable flexibility.

- **Move from tenure to contracts for service.** We explained earlier our concern that tenure gets in the way of organizations being nimble, responsive and able to change their business model. Freedom of expression, which is why tenure came about, can be protected in other ways. Tenure should go and be placed by outcome based, time limited (but renewable) performance contracts.

- **Adopt results based management and budgeting.** If there is to be a shift from funding based on the Carnegie unit (time served by students for credit) towards block funding and if we are to focus the work of institutions on achieving impact, then results based management and evaluation become the bedrock of assurance and accountability. From experience, we see very little use of the disciplined and systematic use of RBM in colleges and universities. For example, find a logic model or an outputs – outcome table in any annual report. It is time for a serious rethink of how we ensure that these organizations are focused on what matters most.

These thirteen developments, coupled with the twelve from the previous list, amount to major innovative and structural change in our post-secondary education system. But these will matter little if we do not address the third area of change which is urgent: How students are taught and how they learn.

3. Enabling Pedagogic Innovation

The single largest challenge in post-secondary education is to ensure that the experience students have of learning is so powerful and compelling that it changes how they think, feel and behave. It not only provides them with the specific knowledge, understanding and skill associated with a particular competency, course or program but does so in a way that is mindful, memorable and compelling.

Decades of research shows us that student engagement in their learning is the critical variable in determining the outcomes of that learning. While their knowledge and skill level on entering a learning task matter, a more powerful force in determining outcomes is motivation – open learning institutions repeatedly demonstrate that learners with poor previous learning performance can excel if they are driven to do so and receive appropriate and engaging support. Since life-long learning is so critical to the wellbeing of individuals, community and the economy, ensuring that learners have a compelling, powerful and engaged learning experience in every class, course and program should be mission critical for our colleges, universities, training organizations and polytechnics. It is not[57].

Many college staff, especially in trade schools, receive no training in instructional design or teaching. They are hired because of their expertise and practical knowledge of the subjects they teach. In colleges and universities, the focus on the PhD as a requirement for hiring is also about subject matter knowledge and expertise – few (if any) doctoral programs spend any serious time helping candidates understand what excellence in teaching and learning looks like. If we are to take our public investment and social responsibilities seriously, we need to take a hard look at teaching and learning as the key challenge in rethinking post-secondary education. Many recognize this – there is a major project in Australia rethinking how college and university teachers are evaluated, for example,[58] as well as an international study of student engagement[59] - but it is time for concerted action.

Here are our suggestions:

- **During the hiring process for faculty, explore the model of learning and teaching candidates hold.** In addition to ensuring that the candidate has the appropriate subject knowledge, a substantial portion of the recruitment process should focus on how the candidate envisages teaching and learning and what support they will need to improve their abilities to facilitate engaged learning. Ideally, we should seek a demonstration of their teaching (either in vivo, on video or through some other means) or at least secure lesson plans for two or three different teaching challenges related to their subject as part of the recruitment process.

- **On hiring, develop a professional development and learning contract focused on improving their understanding of pedagogy.** Most of the conversation immediately after hiring focuses on content issues, time-table, access to services and formal requirements. Little time is spent on teaching and learning and how this can be improved. Post-secondary institutions should focus a great deal of effort and attention on what each new hire needs in terms of professional development to enable them to become outstanding teachers.

- **Moving from tenure to contracts for service enables a strong focus on learning and learning outcomes as contractual obligations.** The abolition of tenure or life-time employment through seniority and the move to contracts should be used as an opportunity to contractually specific a learning focused teaching requirement as measured by both process indicators (how teaching is done) and outcome measures (what the results are).

- **All new hires should be required, within their first year of work, to complete both an in class and an online professional development activity and be paid for doing so.** Many institutions offer focused and high quality professional development opportunities for faculty and many new faculty members appear keen to pursue them. Here they will see examples of different approaches to teaching and learning and begin to understand approaches which leverage technology for blended learning and the "flipped" classroom. But they also need to understand how they design, develop and deploy online learning resources which make extensive use of open education resources (OER)[60]. Capacity building is a critical task for our institutions.

- **During the first year peer observation should take place.** As a new hire a colleague should be assigned to mentor, coach and guide the faculty member with a focus on learning and teaching – providing feedback and guidance on effective teaching and engaged learning.

- **Assessment of teaching should be required for all who teach.** Currently some basic data from student satisfaction questionnaires and output data are used to "assess" teaching. Few institutions take a systematic and rigorous approach to this work, based on student engagement, service or peer review of teaching as an activity. This needs to change. If we are to secure major gains in productivity as well as to embrace effective teaching, institutions need to become much more rigorous in evaluating and improving their core asset: instructional quality.

- **Courses and programs should be redesigned as modules focused on competencies and learning outcomes.** The redesign of courses based on instructional design is a critical requirement for moving from a closed and limited entry system to a more open, year round admission system. Using instructional design, modern analytics and appropriate learning strategies for each module becomes a means by which institutions can define their approach to learning. Some modules may not need instructional support – they can be mastered "as is" by learners. Some may need intensive instructional support. One size and one approach to learning and instruction will not fit all.

- **Students should be actively involved in learning design**. Students are experts in how students learn, yet we rarely ask them to help us improve the design of the learning we provide to them. We should. Not all students should be involved, but we need to develop a cadre of reflective learners who can help advance learning.

- **Assessment of learning should be redesigned**. New developments in assessment[61], which make use of computer based assessments and neural networks, permit complex assessment tools to be used to develop comprehensive assessments available online 365 days a year. Students can complete an assessment anytime, anywhere and receive instant feedback as to their strengths and weaknesses and receive appropriate resources that enable them to undertake remedial learning to improve their performance (this is known as adaptive learning resourcing). While this facilitates engaged assessment, it also provides strong analytics for individualized interventions by instructors to support learning.

- **Learning should be seen as an individual process not a "batch function"**. Sir Ken Robinson is fond of suggesting that most learning is based on a batch processing/ factor model. It no longer need be. While we can still have 250 person classes (Sir Ken frequently presents to much larger audiences), we can also use smart assessment and adaptive learning resourcing to enable much more personalized instruction and support.

- **Learners should proceed through courses and programs at their own pace**. Shifting from a small number of fixed entry points to courses starting 365 days of the year changes not just the business model but the nature of instructions. As learners progress through their learning, class activities, online learning and 1:1 or small seminar activities become milestone activities. Most of the teaching will be done through blended learning and most of the learner support will be done online, by telephone, by videoconference or in person. Not all courses will be offered 365 days a year – lab classes or those requiring access to simulators or equipment might be scheduled to run four or five times a year. But as more of the learning can be done independently of the faculty time-table, instruction can shift from "chalk and talk" to mentoring, coaching and guiding. We can see this in action at the Khan Academy.

- **Reward and recognition should be linked to student engagement and learning outcomes**. Continued employment depends in part on teaching performance, but the evidence based for these decisions is not as robust as it might be – a point made strongly by the Auditor General of Ontario in their review of teaching quality[62]. A more rigorous approach to this dimension of the performance contract is required.

These twelve suggestions point to a rethink of how we hire, support, evaluate and enable those who teach as well as a rethinking of the way in which we structure the experience of learning. These are major changes, but critical if we want to transform education beyond school.

Conclusion

In this section we suggest a total of thirty seven changes which, in our view, would transform post-secondary education and lead to higher education being more focused, efficient and effective. It would also lead to a greater degree of affordable access to student focused quality learning, anytime and anywhere. These changes would also enable the development of systems focused on equity and leverage all of the resources of a community – public and private – in the service of that community's future. While readers may not agree with all of these suggestions, our purpose was to engage the conversation and enable a dialogue on what change needs to look like in the service of equity.

It's a noble challenge. Other voices are promoting different conceptions of education at the post-secondary level and are challenging communities and governments to adopt a market-based and competitive paradigm – a paradigm fraught with difficulty. It is fast becoming time for courageous leadership. This book should help leaders have a bold conversation about their model for the future of post-secondary education.

References and Resources

Preface

[1] Friedman, T (2013) Revolution Hits the Universities. New York Times, January 26th 2013 at http://www.nytimes.com/2013/01/27/opinion/sunday/friedman-revolution-hits-the-universities.html?pagewanted=2&_r=2&

[2] Barber, M., Donnely, K and Rizvi, S (2013) *An Avalanche is Coming – Higher Education and the Revolution Ahead*. London: Institute for Public Policy Research (mimeo). March available at http://www.ippr.org/publication/55/10432/an-avalanche-is-coming-higher-education-and-the-revolution-ahead

[3] Murgatroyd, S. and Thomas, S. (1974) *Education Beyond School*. London: Fabian Society.

[4] See Conference Board briefing at http://www.conferenceboard.ca/topics/immigration/default.aspx

Five Game Changing Developments for Education Beyond School

[5] http://www.edmontonjournal.com/news/alberta-politics/viz/ministry/index.html, accessed June 17, 2013.

[6] See http://www.worldsalaries.org/professor.shtml

[7] See http://www.washingtonmonthly.com/magazine/septemberoctober_2011/features/administrators_ate_my_tuition031641.php?page=all, accessed June 17, 2013

[8] http://mtprof.msun.edu/Win1992/berg.html accessed June 17, 2013

[9] http://www.telegraph.co.uk/education/educationnews/9074040/Dozens-of-university-heads-take-salary-rises-of-up-to-30pc.html, accessed June 17, 2013

[10] See, for example, a description of their strategies and investments across the Commonwealth at http://www.col.org/progServ/programmes/education/higherEd/Pages/default.aspx

[11] For a listing, see the Financial Times listing at http://rankings.ft.com/businessschoolrankings/directory

[12] See http://www.col.org/resources/publications/Pages/detail.aspx?PID=354 for a summary and report.

[13] See http://www.engc.org.uk/education--skills/engineering-education-and-skills for details.

[14] See Larsen, P.O. and Ins, M. (2010) The rate of growth in scientific publication and the decline in coverage provided by Science Citation Index. *Scientometrics*. Vol 84(3): 575–603

[15] For a complete review of climategate resources, see http://www.climategate.com/

[16] See http://rogerpielkejr.blogspot.ca/2012/11/i-am-roughly-18-feet-tall-critque-of.html for Roger Pielke Jr.'s discussion of this PNAS article.

[17] This robust scientific debate can be looked at here: http://rogerpielkejr.blogspot.ca/2010/06/peter-webster-on-pnas-paper-very-likely.html

[18] See Paul Krugman's blog for accounts of these disputes – for example, http://krugman.blogs.nytimes.com/2013/07/06/regions-of-derpistan/ is not an unusual entry. There are many more.

[19] We are grateful to Dr Pasi Sahlberg (Director General of CIMO, Finland) for his introduction to this term.

[20] See http://www.unesco.org/new/en/education/themes/leading-the-international-agenda/rethinking-education/mission/
[21] See http://unesdoc.unesco.org/images/0010/001095/109590eo.pdf

Six Big Distractions

[22] You can read more about Gartner's methodology at
http://www.gartner.com/technology/research/methodologies/hype-cycle.jsp
[23] September 25th edition available at
http://www.theglobeandmail.com/news/national/education/university-education-no-guarantee-of-earnings-success/article4182805/
[24] See Megan McArdle, *Newsweek* September 17, 2012
[25] See http://www4.hrsdc.gc.ca/.3ndic.1t.4r@-eng.jsp?iid=54
[26] See Read more: http://www.insidehighered.com/news/2013/06/26/oecd-education-glance-report-considers-relationship-between-recession-education-and#ixzz2ZbV3MAuX
[27] Study is available at
http://notes.ocufa.on.ca/OCUFARsrch.nsf/9da1693cdc3d700f852573db006561fc/ee3155f49ece230d852573db006b0945/$FILE/funding_postsecondary.pdf
[28] Harden, N (2013) The End of the University as we Know It. *The American Interest*, Jan/Feb at http://www.the-american-interest.com/article.cfm?piece=1352
[29] See Christensen, C. and Eyring, H.J. (2011) How Disruptive Innovation is Remaking the University. *HBR Working Knowledge* at http://hbswk.hbs.edu/item/6746.html
[30] See http://www.ed.psu.edu/educ/cshe/working-papers/WP%236
[31] But see http://www.marcprensky.com/blog/archives/000045.html
[32] See Pettigrew, T (2012) Digital Natives – Not My Students *Maclean's*, September 2012 at http://oncampus.macleans.ca/education/2012/12/07/digital-natives-not-my-students/
[33] Harden, N (2013) *op.cit*

Four Scenarios for Change

[34] This is an important caveat. The scenarios here are all based on Europe and North America and would not apply to many developing countries.
[35] Oxford is being sued for failing to ensure access to a qualified candidate who is deemed "poor" – see http://www.telegraph.co.uk/education/universityeducation/9814000/Oxford-college-sued-for-discriminating-against-the-poor.html See also
http://world.time.com/2013/01/08/can-oxbridge-solve-its-privilege-problem/
[36] See Sloan Consortium (2012) at
http://sloanconsortium.org/publications/survey/changing_course_2012
[37] Can Essays be Graded by Artificial Intelligence? International Herald Tribune, April 6-7th 2013.
[38] *ibid*
[39] See, for example, the 2007 from the Council of Ministers of Education, Canada at http://www.cicic.ca/docs/cmec/QA-Statement-2007.en.pdf
[40] See
http://europa.eu/legislation_summaries/education_training_youth/general_framework/ef0016_en.htm

[41] Since 1994 the SAT has been for "scholastic assessment" but was initially names scholastic assessment.

[42] But this is in part due to the development of degree programs in colleges and second tier (new) universities, enabling a redistribution of the total population of undergraduate and college applications. See Casas, F.R. and Meaghan, D.E. (1995) Grade Inflation and University Admission in Ontario – Separating Fact from Perception. Canadian Journal of Higher Education, Vol 25(3) available at http://ojs.library.ubc.ca/index.php/cjhe/article/view/183222/183186

[43] The full article is available at http://www.theatlantic.com/magazine/archive/2005/11/does-meritocracy-work/304305/

[44] The current UK cabinet is led by a group of sixteen members who all went to Oxford and Cambridge and who also appear to be "at war" with those least able to cope with modern living. Michael Young may have written a novel, but fiction has a habit of becoming fact.

[45] Data from Statistics Canada at http://www.statcan.gc.ca/pub/81-004-x/2010002/article/11253-eng.htm

[46] Zakaria, F. (2013) The Thin Envelope Crisis. CNN Podcast / Time Magazine April 15th 2013 available at http://www.time.com/time/magazine/article/0,9171,2140209,00.html

[47] ibid

[48] See, for example, http://www.bbc.co.uk/news/education-12914964

Seven Key Considerations for Decision Makers

[49] http://www.cbc.ca/news/business/story/2008/05/15/f-highereducation-tuitionfees.html

[50] For more information, see http://www.open.edu.au/about-us/who-we-are/

[51] See, for example, http://www.open.ac.uk/cobe/docs/COBE-WBL-booklet.pdf and also http://www.heacademy.ac.uk/assets/documents/research/wbl_illuminating.pdf

[52] See http://articles.washingtonpost.com/2009-04-19/opinions/36825345_1_professors-academic-freedom-economics

[53] See
http://www.otherworldsarepossible.org/sites/default/files/documents/who%20says%20you%20cant%20change%20the%20world_1.pdf

The Three Big Enabling Opportunities for Rethinking Post-Secondary Education

[54] See http://learnondemand.kctcs.edu/ for a description of learn on demand and the modular approach.

[55] See, for example,
http://www.wiche.edu/info/publications/ntnmStateCaseStudiesExecSum.pdf

[56] Henley is now integrated with the University of Reading.

[57] For a study of what happens now, see a review of teaching quality in Ontario conducted by the Provincial auditor at http://www.auditor.on.ca/en/reports_en/en12/312en12.pdf

[58] See http://www.oecd.org/site/eduimhe08/41216416.pdf

[59] The National Survey of Student Engagement (NSSE) – pioneered in the US and adopted in Canada, modified for use in Australia and New Zealand (as AUSSE) and South Africa (as SASSE), and currently being piloted in China and the UK. See

http://www.heacademy.ac.uk/assets/documents/studentengagement/StudentEngagementE
videnceSummary.pdf

[60] For a guide to OER resources see the excellent guide produced by the Commonwealth of Learning – available at
http://www.col.org/resources/publications/Pages/detail.aspx?PID=357

[61] See the work of the Centre for Research in Applied Measurement and Evaluation at the University of Alberta, for example -
http://www2.education.ualberta.ca/educ/psych/crame/research.html

[62] op.cit – see note 57 above.